Wild

France Royer &
Richard Dickinson

flowers
of Edmonton
and Central
Alberta

The
University
of Alberta
Press

Published by
The University of Alberta Press
Athabasca Hall
Edmonton, Alberta
Canada T6G 2E8

Printed in Canada 5 4 3 2 1

ISBN 0–88864–282-2

Canadian Cataloguing in Publication Data

Royer, France, 1951–
    Wildflowers of Edmonton and Central Alberta

    Includes bibliographical references and index.
    ISBN 0–88864–282–2

    1. Wild flowers—Alberta—Edmonton—Identification. 2. Wild flowers—
Alberta—Edmonton. 3. Wild flowers—Alberta—Identification. 4. Wild flowers—
Alberta. I. Dickinson, Richard, 1960– II. Title.
QK203.A3R69 1996   582.13'097123'34   C96-910497-9

∞ Printed on acid-free paper.

Color separations and filmwork by Resistance Graphics, Edmonton, Canada.
Printed and bound by Quality Color Press, Edmonton, Canada.

COMMITTED TO THE DEVELOPMENT OF CULTURE AND THE ARTS

The publisher gratefully aknowledges the assistance of the Department of
Canadian Heritage.

WARNING

*The uses of plants discussed in this field guide are not in any way recommendations
by the authors or the publisher. Readers are cautioned against using these plants as
food or for self-medication. Notes about potential plant toxicity or irritating side
effects have been highlighted in the following descriptions, but we recommend
caution with ALL plants, especially those unfamiliar to you.*

Table of Contents

In Memory of Alice (Fortin) Royer

Acknowledgements

*T*he authors would like to thank Lynn Milne and Cathy Cross for their editing and constructive suggestions, and friends and family who provided moral support and encouragement throughout the production of this field guide.

We also would like to thank Edmonton Nature Centres' Foundation and Weyerhaeuser Canada Ltd. for their financial support in the publishing of this book.

prairie crocus (page 22)

above: marsh ragwort (page 10)
opposite: Canada anemone (page 21)

Foreword

*F*rance Royer and Richard Dickinson have created an informative, user-friendly plant guide for the Edmonton area. An interest in wildflowers is all that is needed to use this book.

Wildflowers of Edmonton and Central Alberta helps self-taught naturalists to identify wildflower species easily and accurately by checking clearly recognizable features. Photos help confirm each identification. Each species description also includes comments on historical, medicinal and commercial uses of the plant.

The realm of science reaches far beyond any single text; it accumulates lifetimes of dedication and study. *Wildflowers of Edmonton and Central Alberta* is a fun and friendly introduction.

The aims of the Foundation are to support the John Janzen Nature Centre and its staff, and to foster an appreciation of nature in the Edmonton area. *Wildflowers* captured the interest of the Foundation Board, and we are delighted to assist with its publication.

**EDMONTON NATURE
CENTRES' FOUNDATION**

DAVE MCINNES
JIM RYAN
*on behalf of the
Edmonton Nature
Centres' Foundation*

top: wild red currant (page 31)
bottom left: baneberry (page 20)
bottom right: blue columbine (page 23)
opposite: wild blue flax (page 39)

Introduction

Wildflowers of Edmonton and Central Alberta is a handy field guide to the plants in Edmonton and central Alberta. The area is mainly aspen parkland but has small pockets of prairie grassland, black spruce muskeg and pine-dominated sand ridges. These habitats feature more than 750 species of plants, large and small, including many showy wildflowers.

Thirty-three plant families, with descriptions of 145 common or unusual species, are included in this guide. A simple identification key allows naturalists of all ages to recognize common features easily; line drawings are included to aid identification. Descriptions explain when and where to look for a plant, its identifying features and closely related species. Two hundred and six colour photographs complement the descriptions.

Plants in this guide are grouped in families, listed alphabetically by common family name. Within each family, species are listed alphabetically by scientific name but also identified by common names. Species belonging to the same family share similar characteristics, such as flower structure and leaf arrangement.

Species featured in this book can be viewed while travelling throughout the region, whether walking, cycling or hiking. An ethnobotanical section, included for most species, explains how plants were used by natives and pioneers, and how they are used today. The guide is designed to be both informative and entertaining, encouraging readers to learn more about the ecology of Central Alberta.

WARNING

The uses of plants discussed in this field guide are not in any way recommendations by the authors or the publisher. Readers are cautioned against using these plants as food or for self-medication. Notes about potential plant toxicity or irritating side effects have been highlighted in the following descriptions, but we recommend caution with ALL plants, especially those unfamiliar to you.

Map of
Central Alberta

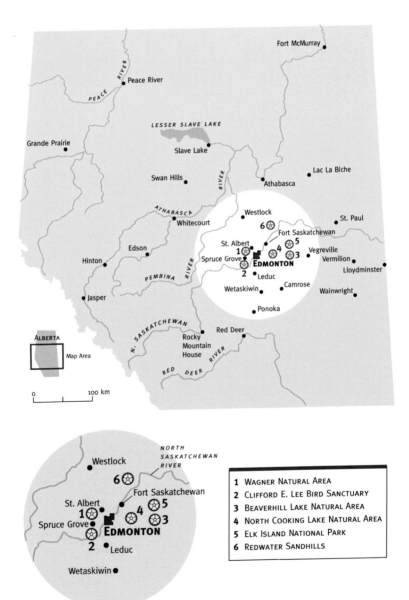

1 WAGNER NATURAL AREA
2 CLIFFORD E. LEE BIRD SANCTUARY
3 BEAVERHILL LAKE NATURAL AREA
4 NORTH COOKING LAKE NATURAL AREA
5 ELK ISLAND NATIONAL PARK
6 REDWATER SANDHILLS

Where to Find Wildflowers
in Central Alberta

THE CITY OF EDMONTON

The North Saskatchewan River winds its way through the City of Edmonton. Parks created by Edmonton Parks and Recreation line both sides of this 40 km stretch of valley. More than 150 km of bicycle trails and walking paths have been constructed for the enjoyment of Edmontonians and visitors. These paths travel through a variety of habitats. The cool, moist north-facing slopes are dominated by white spruce forest, whose species composition differs greatly from the drier, aspen-grassland south-facing slopes.

ELK ISLAND NATIONAL PARK

is located 40 km east of Edmonton on Highway 16. The park and wildlife refuge was created in 1913, primarily for the plains and wood bison. More than 350 species of vascular plants have been identified in this 194 km² area. The 80 km of hiking trails take the outdoor enthusiast through various habitats, including wetlands, sandhills and aspen parkland.

NORTH COOKING LAKE NATURAL AREA

is located 20 km east of Sherwood Park. Its habitats and plant species composition are similar to those found in Elk Island National Park. Wild birds and larger mammals can be viewed from the hiking trails.

BEAVERHILL LAKE NATURAL AREA

is located 10 km east of Tofield. This natural area includes the Pelican and Dekker Islands and the southeast shoreline of Beaverhill Lake, an excellent area for watching migratory and shoreline birds. The soil in this wetland area is strongly alkaline, allowing salt-tolerant plant species to thrive. Small pockets of aspen parkland are also present in this area.

REDWATER SANDHILLS

are located to the north and west of Redwater. Drought-tolerant species such as bearberry, sand heather and jack pine are common here. Most sandhill plant species bloom in April and May while moisture is still readily available.

WAGNER NATURAL AREA

is located 7 km west of Edmonton, southwest of the junction of Highway 16X and Highway 794. Designated a natural area in 1975, this 400-acre parcel of land boasts 300 species of vascular plants. 16 of Alberta's 24 species of orchids are found here. Trails wander through several types of habitat: marl ponds, sedge wetland meadows and white spruce forest. Note: Please stay on the trails and boardwalks. Calcareous peatlands are fragile habitats and do not recover from human disturbance.

CLIFFORD E. LEE BIRD SANCTUARY

is located north of Devon, 3 km west of Highway 60 on Woodbend Road. This sanctuary is an important staging area for migratory birds. The wetlands, interspersed with pine-dominated sandhills, are great for birdwatching and for viewing aquatic and emergent vegetation.

Plant Structures

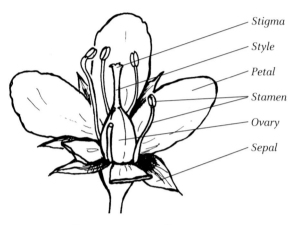

Stigma
Style
Petal
Stamen
Ovary
Sepal

CROSS-SECTION OF A FLOWER

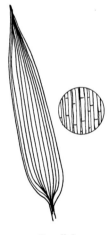

Net–veined
(pinnate)

Parallel

LEAF VENATION

Simple

*Palmately
Compound*

*Trifoliately
Compound*

*Pinnately
Compound*

LEAF TYPE

How to Use this Key

Answer question 1 to determine which leaf arrangement the plant exhibits. Proceed to the table or page number listed below the corresponding line drawing.

STEP 2

Select the appropriate habitat, growth habit or number of leaves as indicated in the first column of the table.

STEP 3

Choose the distinguishing characteristics that best describe the plant.

STEP 4

Proceed to the page numbers listed after the family name and compare the specimen with the photographs and text on those pages.

Note: Remember not all species are included in this field guide.

top left: round-leaved hawthorn (page 90)
top right: ostrich fern (page 37)
bottom left: round-leaved sundew (page 100)
bottom right: three-toothed cinquefoil (page 92)

Key to Plant Families

QUESTION 1

Which leaf arrangement does your plant exhibit?

ALTERNATE
Tables 1 & 2
Pages xviii–xx

OPPOSITE
Table 3
Page xxi

BASAL
Table 4
Page xxii

WHORLED
Table 5
Page xxiii

BUNDLES
Table 2
Page xx

Plants with Alternate Leaves

Does your plant have a soft or woody stem?

Soft Stems – *see **Table 1: Herbaceous Plants.***

Woody Stems – *see **Table 2: Trees and Shrubs.***

TABLE 1

Herbaceous Plants with Alternate Leaves

Habitat	Distinguishing Characteristics	Family (page #)
open areas	climbing plants; leaves simple	Morning Glory (69)
	climbing plants; leaves compound	Pea (76-82)
	compound leaves with 3 leaflets	Pea (76-82)
	flowers blue with a yellow center	Borage (17-18)
	flowers yellow with an orange spot	Figwort (38)
	leaves parallel veined; petals white	Lily (60-64)
	petals more than 10	Aster (3-13)
	petals blue with dark veins	Flax (39)
	petals blue; flowers bell-shaped	Harebell (43)
	petals 4, pink; flowers less than 1 cm across	Mustard (70)
	petals purple; dry habitat	Violet (101)
	plants yellowish-green; stems with milky juice	Spurge (99)

Habitat	Distinguishing Characteristics	Family (page #)
wet areas	aquatic plant; petals pink	*Buckwheat (19)*
	compound leaves with 5 or more leaflets; petals white	*Carrot (27-28)*
	compound leaves with 3 leaflets; petals pink	*Rose (89-97)*
	petals yellow, pouch-like; leaves parallel veined	*Orchid (73-75)*
	petals more than 10; stems hairy	*Aster (3-13)*
woodlands	compound leaves; plants not hairy	*Buttercup (20-26)*
	compound leaves with 3 large leaflets; petals white	*Carrot (27-28)*
	simple leaves with 3 veins; petals pink	*Evening Primrose (36)*
	leaves parallel veined; petals white	*Lily (60-64)*
	petals blue; flower buds pink; leaves hairy	*Borage (17-18)*
	petals white; leaves heart-shaped	*Violet (101)*

Table 2

Woody Plants with Alternate Leaves

Growth Habit	Distinguishing Characteristics	Family (page #)
shrub	compound leaves with 8, 10 or 12 leaflets	*Pea (76-82)*
	compound leaves with 5, 7, 9 or 11 leaflets	*Rose (89-97)*
	leaves with jagged edges; bark brown or grey	*Birch (14-16)*
	leaves maple leaf-shaped, edges jagged	*Currant (30-31)*
	leaves leathery and evergreen; shrub less than 0.5 m tall	*Heath (44-49)*
	leaves silver-coloured; petals 4, yellow	*Oleaster (71-72)*
	leaves and stems hairy; sandy habitats only	*Rockrose (88)*
	petals 5, white; fruit red or purplish-black	*Rose (89-97)*
tree	leaves with jagged edges; bark papery	*Birch (14-16)*
	leaves needle-like; bark grey and rough	*Pine (83-85)*
	leaves with smooth edges; bark green	*Willow (102-103)*

TABLE 3
Plants with Opposite Leaves

Growth Habit	Distinguishing Characteristics	Family (page #)
climbing vine	compound leaves with 3 or 5 leaflets; leaf stalks twisting	*Buttercup (20-26)*
	simple leaves; stems twisting	*Honeysuckle (50-57)*
soft stems	grows on the branches of pines	*Mistletoe (68)*
	petals white with purple veins; leaves lobed	*Geranium (40)*
	stems with milky juice; petals pink	*Dogbane (32)*
	stems square; flowers purple or pink	*Mint (66-67)*
shrub	leaf underside green; petals 5, white, orange or yellow	*Honeysuckle (50-57)*
	leaf underside brown dotted; petals 4, yellowish-brown	*Oleaster (71-72)*
	red bark; petals 4, white	*Dogwood (33-34)*

TABLE 4
Plants with Basal Leaves

Habitat	Distinguishing Characteristics	Family (page #)
open areas	compound leaf with 3 leaflets	*Rose (89-97)*
	petals purple; leaves grass-like	*Iris (59)*
wet areas	1 stem leaf; petals 5, white	*Grass-of-Parnassus (42)*
	1 basal leaf (inconspicuous in Coral-root)	*Orchid (73-75)*
	free floating aquatic plant; leaves with roots	*Duckweed (35)*
	leaves horseshoe or palm-shaped; petals more than 10	*Aster (3-13)*
	leaves spongy; flowers brownish-green	*Cattail (29)*
	leaves with sticky-tipped hairs	*Sundew (100)*
	petals turned back or leaves dusty-powdered	*Primrose (86-87)*
	white petal-like leaf surrounding flowering stalk	*Arum (2)*
woodlands	4 to 6 compound leaves; flowering stalk brownish-green	*Fern (37)*
	compound leaves with 3 leaflets; edges jagged	*Rose (89-97)*
	plant with the scent of onion; petals pink	*Lily (60-64)*
	flowers white in globe-shaped clusters; single compound leaf with 9 to 15 leaflets	*Ginseng (41)*
	leaves bristly; 1 stem leaf; petals yellow	*Saxifrage (98)*
	leaves round and evergreen; petals 5, pink	*Wintergreen (104)*

TABLE 5
Plants with Whorled Leaves

Leaves Per Whorl	Distinguishing Characteristics	Family (page #)
2 to 5	petals 5 to 9, white or pale blue; leaves hairy	Buttercup (20-26)
4 to 6	leaves net veined; flowers with 4 large white "petals"	Dogwood (33-34)
4	stems square; flowers white	Madder (65)
5 to 8	leaves parallel veined; petals orange with black spots	Lily (60-64)
8 to 16	stems jointed and hollow	Horsetail (58)

Plant Descriptions

Individual plant descriptions follow on pages 2–104.

top: bog rosemary (page 44)
bottom left: harebell (page 43)
bottom right: long-fruited anemone (page 21)

water arum, wild calla

Calla palustris L.

WHERE, WHEN AND WHAT TO LOOK FOR

Wild arum grows in boggy sloughs and along lakeshores in Central Alberta, including Elk Island National Park. Flowers appear from **June to July** on a stalk surrounded by a large (2.5 to 4 cm long), **white, leaf-like bract called a 'spathe.'** Sepals and petals are absent. Basal leaves are parallel-veined and about 5 to 10 cm long. Leaves and flowering stalks grow from an underwater stem which has roots which may be free-floating or affixed in mud or muskeg. Red, berry-like fruit appear in August and contain only a few seeds.

DID YOU KNOW...

The Cree pulverized the roots and used the mash in bread-making.

yarrow

Achillea millefolium L.

WHERE, WHEN AND WHAT TO LOOK FOR

Yarrow commonly grows in prairie grassland, roadside ditches, and waste areas throughout our region. Flower heads appear from **June to August.** They are composed of 10 to 30 yellow disc florets, and 5 to 12 sterile, white or pinkish white ray florets. The woolly-haired stem, which can grow up to 80 cm, has alternate leaves which are 4 to 15 cm long and feathered into numerous 1 to 2 mm wide segments (giving the species its name, *millefolium,* meaning 'thousand leaves'). The fruit is a flattened achene with no pappus.

DID YOU KNOW ...

The genus *Achillea* is named after the Greek hero Achilles, who is said to have used yarrow to treat the wounds of his soldiers. Natives and herbalists continued to use this medicinal herb. The Cree treated ear-aches, constipation, stomach ailments, burns and infections with yarrow. A tea made from yarrow and strawberries was taken to treat insanity. A yarrow shampoo was used to prevent baldness. Dried yarrow leaves and flowers added to a warm bath have been used to relieve arthritic pain.

common burdock
Arctium minus (Hill) Bernh.

WHERE, WHEN AND WHAT TO LOOK FOR

Common burdock was introduced from Europe and is now found in waste places, railway grades and edges of wooded areas throughout the Central Alberta. Flowers appear from **July to August** as heads (1 to 3 cm thick) of pinkish purple disc florets enclosed in several series of bracts bearing hooked prickles. The plant grows to a height of 2 m, with large basal leaves and alternate leaves that can grow up to 50 cm long and 40 cm wide. The leaf underside appears pale due to a mass of woolly hairs. The fruit, a small, dry, single seed, does not open when ripe. It is 5 to 6 mm long, has 3 to 5 angles, and a bristly pappus. Each flowering head produces several 1-seeded fruits.

SIMILAR SPECIES

A closely related species, woolly burdock (*A. tomentosum* Mill.), can occasionally be found in the Edmonton area. Its flower has dense, woolly bracts.

DID YOU KNOW ...

The Japanese cultivate burdock as a prized vegetable. The fleshy taproot of first-year plants, called 'Gobo,' can be eaten raw or cooked. The root, ground and roasted, serves as a coffee substitute. The leaves, flowering stalks and seeds are all edible.

plains wormwood

pasture sagewort
Artemisia frigida Willd.

WHERE, WHEN AND WHAT TO LOOK FOR

The pasture sagewort is found on dry, south-facing riverbanks and overgrazed pastures and prairie. Small flower heads appear from **July to August.** They are composed of small, yellow disc florets enclosed by hairy bracts. The small flowers are hidden along leafy, woody stalks which can grow to a height of 50 cm. Alternate, silvery-green leaves grow 1 to 3 cm long, dissected into narrow segments. The leaves give off the distinct scent of sage, especially if you rub them between your fingers. The fruit is an achene, 3 mm long and without a pappus.

SIMILAR SPECIES

A closely related species, plains wormwood (*A. campestris* L.), has aromatic leaves and is found in dry, sandy areas. The stems of this plant are usually reddish.

DID YOU KNOW...

Pasture sagewort has many uses. The Blackfoot chewed the leaves to relieve heartburn, and they used the leaves to brew a tea as a remedy for coughs and colds. Trappers used the aromatic leaves as bait in their traps. Leaves can be used as a stuffing or seasoning when fresh or dried, and they add a natural perfume to sachets or pot-pourri. Leaves tossed into a campfire will produce a pleasant fragrance.

pasture sagewort

showy aster

Aster conspicuus Lindl.

showy aster

WHERE, WHEN AND WHAT TO LOOK FOR

Showy aster is found on the edges of aspen forests and moist, roadside ditches. Flower heads (3 to 4 cm wide) appear from **August to September.** They are composed of pale-purple to pink ray florets and yellowish brown disc florets. The rough-textured stem rises up to 1 m from a large rootstock. The alternate leaves, which grow up to 15 cm long and 7 cm wide, are also rough-textured. The fruit is an achene with many white hairs.

SIMILAR SPECIES

A closely related species, smooth aster (*A. laevis* L.), has smaller, pinkish white flower heads. Plains peoples sometimes used the smoke of the burning plant to revive an unconscious patient.

DID YOU KNOW...

The aster is held sacred by some native peoples and has been used as medicine to ward off snakes. The native peoples of Alberta used the stems, leaves, and flowers to make a dye.

smooth aster

Canada thistle

Cirsium arvense (L.) Scop.

WHERE, WHEN AND WHAT TO LOOK FOR

Canada thistle is a deep-rooted perennial commonly found in large patches in roadside ditches, waste areas and cultivated fields throughout our region. Male and female flower heads, composed of purplish pink disc florets (each 2 to 3 mm wide), bloom on separate plants from **July to September.** The stems can grow to a height of 1.5 m and have alternate leaves 5 to 15 cm long, with prickly lobed segments. The fruit is an achene with a white, feathery pappus.

DID YOU KNOW...

A plaster made from boiled thistle roots has been used as a deodorant. The cottony seeds have been stuffed into pillows, cushions and mattresses. The young leaves and roots of Canada thistle make an excellent vegetable. Livestock will eat Canada thistle when grass is scarce. Herbalists prescribe thistle for treatment of muscle spasms, rickets and nervous disorders. Fresh-cut thistle flowers add a pleasant fragrance to a room and dried flowers can be added to sachets and pot-pourris.

pineapple-weed
Matricaria matricarioides
(Less.) Porter

pineapple-weed

WHERE, WHEN AND WHAT TO LOOK FOR
Pineapple-weed is common in waste areas, roadsides and yards.
The greenish yellow, cone-shaped flower heads are composed of
disc florets. They can be seen from **June through September.**
The plant grows to a height of 40 cm, with numerous branches.
Its alternate leaves (1 to 5 cm long) are each divided into several
narrow segments. Pineapple-weed has a strong pineapple odour.
The fruit is an achene without a hairy pappus.

SIMILAR SPECIES
A closely related species, scentless chamomile (*M. perforata*
Merat), has white ray florets and yellow disc florets. Its leaves
are 2 to 8 cm long, with narrower divisions than those of
pineapple-weed.

DID YOU KNOW...
A tea known for its relaxing effect can be brewed from the
flower heads, leaves and stems of both species. The Blackfoot
used pineapple-weed as a perfume and an insect repellent. Both
species can be added to a hot bath for an aromatic soak.

scentless chamomile

arrow-leaved colt's-foot

Petasites sagittatus (Pursh) A. Gray

WHERE, WHEN AND WHAT TO LOOK FOR

Arrow-leaved colt's-foot can grow to a height of 75 cm in wet meadows and ditches. It can be found throughout our region. Male and female flower heads, usually found on separate plants, bloom from **April through May.** Male and female flowers are composed of white ray and yellowish brown disc florets, and **appear before the leaves.** Leaves are basal, triangular, 10 to 30 cm long and 10 to 20 cm wide. They are greyish green and woolly underneath. The fruit is an achene, 2 to 3 mm in length, with numerous soft, white bristles (a pappus).

SIMILAR SPECIES

A closely related species, palmate-leaved colt's-foot (*P. palmatus* (Ait.) A. Gray), appears in moist woods. Its leaves are 5 to 20 cm wide with 5 to 7 irregularly shaped lobes.

DID YOU KNOW ...

The Cree covered worm-infected wounds with a leaf from this plant. It was believed that the leaf would draw worms away from the wound. A syrup made of the leaves, water and honey has been used to treat coughs and colds. The young flowering stalks can be cooked as a spring vegetable.

marsh ragwort

Senecio congestus

(R.Br.) DC.

WHERE, WHEN AND WHAT TO LOOK FOR

An annual, the marsh ragwort blooms from **June through July**, often forming a yellow band along shorelines of lakes, sloughs and streams. In Central Alberta, it can be seen in the North Saskatchewan River valley, Elk Island National Park and Wagner Natural Area. Its flower head (1 to 2 cm across) is composed of yellow ray and disc florets. The fleshy, hollow stem grows to a height of 60 cm, with alternate leaves, 5 to 15 cm in length, that are wavy-margined and woolly. Densely hairy when young, the plants become glabrous as they mature. The achenes have 5 to 10 prominent ribs and many white bristles.

SIMILAR SPECIES

A closely related species, common groundsel (*S. vulgaris* L.), is common in gardens and waste areas. The plant is glabrous and has smaller yellow flowers.

mountain goldenrod

Canada goldenrod

Solidago canadensis L.

WHERE, WHEN AND WHAT TO LOOK FOR

Canada goldenrod, recognizable by its bright-yellow flowers, is common in areas ranging from open meadows to the edges of aspen forests. Flower heads appear from **August through September.** They are composed of ray florets, 3 to 6 mm long. The flowering stalk is usually pyramid-shaped. The plant grows up to 1.2 m, with numerous alternate leaves 5 to 10 cm long, each with 3 prominent veins. The fruit is an achene with bristly white hairs.

SIMILAR SPECIES

A closely related species, mountain goldenrod (*S. spathulata* DC.), grows to 40 cm tall and can be found throughout our region. The flower cluster is cylindrical in shape and has bright yellow flowers.

DID YOU KNOW ...

Goldenrod flowers make a bright-yellow dye. This plant was an ingredient for astringents and diuretics, and was sometimes claimed to be a treatment for diphtheria. Young leaves make an excellent addition to salads and can be cooked like spinach. Some natives treated sore throats with a mixture made from grease and mashed leaves.

Canada goldenrod

11

tansy

Tanacetum vulgare L.

WHERE, WHEN AND WHAT TO LOOK FOR

Tansy was introduced from Europe as a garden flower, but thrived and became a weed. It is common in roadside ditches, waste areas and pastures. Each stem has over 200 button-shaped, yellowish orange flower heads (6 to 10 mm across) that bloom from **July through September.** The plant stem grows up to 180 cm in height and has a pungent odour when crushed. Alternate leaves, up to 20 cm long, are pinnately divided into numerous segments. The fruit is an achene with small ridges and a reduced pappus.

DID YOU KNOW...

Tansy flowers release a fragrant aroma that repels insects. Early farmers on the prairies put the dried flowers in their grain bins to keep mice and other rodents away. Modern herbalists sometimes recommend this plant as a tonic to treat many internal disorders. A skin lotion can be made by soaking the young leaves in buttermilk for about 10 days. Tansy can be **toxic** to humans and caution should be exercised when using any part of this plant.

goat's-beard
Tragopogon dubius Scop.

WHERE, WHEN AND WHAT TO LOOK FOR

Goat's-beard is a weed first introduced from the southwestern United States. In our region it thrives in waste areas, roadside ditches and on railway grades. Its flower heads bloom from **June through August** and are composed of bright-yellow ray florets (up to 6 mm across) and 10 to 14 green involucral bracts that are longer than the ray florets. The stem grows up to 100 cm tall and has a fleshy taproot and milky sap, much like those of the dandelion. Alternate, grass-like leaves grow up to 30 cm in length. Achenes about 25 to 30 mm long have a feather-like pappus, about 4 cm long. The fruiting head of goat's-beard is usually from 7 to 10 cm in diameter.

The flowers of goat's-beard are sensitive to light and temperature. On sunny days the flowers follow the sun; they remain closed on cloudy days.

DID YOU KNOW ...

The roots and leaves of this plant make a pleasant addition to salads. Some people say that the cooked taproot tastes like parsnips or oysters. European settlers and natives both believed that the milky juice dissolved gallstones. Drinking the juice moistens the mouth and is believed by some to promote good digestion.

green alder

Alnus crispa (Ait.) Pursh

green alder

WHERE, WHEN AND WHAT TO LOOK FOR

Green alder grows as a common shrub in sandhills, bogs and dry, open forests. It reaches heights of up to 3 m. Male and female flowers bloom in **April** in separate catkins; female flowers are pinkish purple and the male flowers are yellowish brown. The female catkins—dry cone-like structures 1 to 2 cm long—produce seeds and often remain on the stems for several seasons. Alternate, oval-shaped leaves, 2 to 8 cm long with coarsely serrated leaf margins, **appear with the catkins in early May.**

SIMILAR SPECIES

A closely related species, river alder *(A. tenuifolia* Nutt.*)*, grows up to a height of 8 m and can be found along river banks and lakeshores.

DID YOU KNOW ...

The Blackfoot produced a yellow dye from the catkins of green alder and an orange or reddish brown dye from the inner bark. They boiled the bark with vinegar to make a mouthwash and an excellent remedy for lice, and they also used the bark to to add flavour when they smoked fish and meat. They called the shrub *a-muck-ko-kytis* ('red-mouth bush') because chewing the inner bark turned the mouth red.

river alder with last year's catkins

paper birch, white birch

Betula papyrifera Marsh.

WHERE, WHEN AND WHAT TO LOOK FOR

Paper birch, or white birch, can be found in a variety of habitats from dry sandhills to moist lakeshores throughout Central Alberta. It grows to heights of up to 30 m. It is named for its shredding, papery bark. Young twigs and branches are a reddish brown colour. Male and female catkins, greenish brown in colour, **appear before the leaves in early May.** Alternate leaves, 2 to 8 cm long, have coarsely serrated edges. The fruit, called a 'samara,' takes the form of a single seed surrounded by a thin papery membrane.

DID YOU KNOW ...

Roots, bark, and leaves of the paper birch are edible. Native peoples and early European settlers in the West dried and ground the inner bark into flour. They also cut the inner bark into strips that resembled noodles, boiled it, and added it to stew. The papery outer bark makes a pleasant tea with a caramel aroma. Tea can also be made from the dried leaves and young twigs. The sap can be made into syrup that is not as sweet as its maple counterpart, or into a light beer. Native people used the wood to construct teepees, canoes, snowshoes, eating utensils and baskets. Rotten birch wood provided a reddish dye. The Cree made a body powder from an extract of rotten wood and Labrador tea *(see page 46)*.

beaked hazelnut

Corylus cornuta Marsh.

WHERE, WHEN AND WHAT TO LOOK FOR

Beaked hazelnut is one of the earliest-to-flower plants in Central Alberta. The beaked hazelnut grows commonly in the Edmonton area, mostly in moist aspen forests. Its inconspicuous flower clusters, called 'catkins,' have no sepals or petals. They are easily overlooked because of their size and because they **appear before the leaves, often when snow is still on the ground.** Male and female catkins appear separately on the same plant: the female has 2 to 5 reddish pink pistils about 3 mm long; the male is yellowish brown and 1 to 2 cm long. The number of pistils usually indicates the number of nuts the catkin will produce. The freely branching shrub has mottled-brown bark and oval-shaped, sharply toothed leaves that are 5 to 10 cm long. Beaked hazelnut reaches a height of 3 metres under favourable conditions. The edible nut, which often grows in pairs, is thin-shelled and surrounded by a dense, hairy bract about 3 cm long.

DID YOU KNOW...

The hazelnut is similar to the commercially grown filbert (*C. maxima*). At one time, the Cree collected and stored these nuts, which they call pakan. Human gatherers had to compete with squirrels and chipmunks for this valuable food source. During winters when food is scarce, moose, deer and rabbits feed on the branches of beaked hazlenut.

bluebur

Lappula squarrosa

(Retz.) Dumort.

WHERE, WHEN AND WHAT TO LOOK FOR

Bluebur, a weed introduced from Asia and Europe, inhabits waste areas, railway grades, gardens and roadsides. Its pale, blue flower (about 3 to 6 mm across) has a yellow throat and is borne in leafy clusters. It can be seen **June through September.** An annual, this freely-branching plant is hairy overall and can grow to a height of 50 cm. Alternate greyish green leaves are narrow and up to 7 cm long, and they have numerous stiff hairs. Each flower produces 4 seeds that appear as nutlets with 2 rows of prickles. The seeds' hooked prickles catch on animal fur and clothing, helping them to spread.

DID YOU KNOW...

The genus name, *Lappula*, is Latin for 'small burs.'

lungwort, bluebell

Mertensia paniculata (Ait.) G. Don

WHERE, WHEN AND WHAT TO LOOK FOR

Lungwort, or bluebell, inhabits moist shady areas of aspen groves and spruce forests. It is found throughout our area. The blue, funnel-shaped flower (8 to 14 mm long) has pink petals when in bud. It appears from **June through July.** It blooms in drooping clusters at the ends of the stems. Lungwort grows up to 70 cm tall, has long-stalked basal leaves and dark-green alternate leaves, 5 to 12 cm long, that have prominent veins and are somewhat hairy on both surfaces. Seeds appear as 4 small nutlets enclosed by sepals.

DID YOU KNOW...

The dried leaves and flowers of lungwort can be made into a tea. Fresh lungwort leaves can be added to soups, salads and casseroles.

yard knotweed

water smartweed, lady's-thumb

Polygonum amphibium L.

WHERE, WHEN AND WHAT TO LOOK FOR

Water smartweed, or lady's-thumb, can be found **in the shallow water** of sloughs, ditches and lakeshores. It is found throughout Alberta. Its flowers appear in dense, cylindrical spikes (1 to 3 cm long) from **June through August**. Sepals are pink to reddish purple, 4 to 5 mm long; petals are absent. The water smartweed is a semi-aquatic plant. It sometimes emerges above the water on weak stems that seldom reach beyond 35 cm. Dark-green, alternate leaves are oblong, 2 to 20 cm long and often floating. Fruit is a dry, lens-shaped seed, 2 to 4 mm in length.

SIMILAR SPECIES

A closely related species, yard knotweed (*P. arenastrum* Jord. ex Bor.), is a common weed found in yards, waste places and road-sides. Sepals are green with white or pink margins. Petals are absent.

DID YOU KNOW ...

The Cree applied the crushed fresh root of water smartweed to mouth blisters. Waterfowl, shorebirds and muskrats feed on water smartweed.

water smartweed

baneberry, snake-berry

Actaea rubra (Ait.) Willd.

WHERE, WHEN AND WHAT TO LOOK FOR

A common herb found in aspen and mixed-wood forests, the baneberry, or snake-berry, can be seen throughout our area. White flowers bloom from **May to July.** They consist of 4 to 10 petals and 3 to 5 sepals (which fall off after the flower opens). Flowers are 3 mm across and appear in cone-shaped clusters. Baneberry grows to heights of up to 1 m. Plants have 1 to 5 alternate compound leaves, each with 3 to 7 sharply-toothed leaflets. Showy berries, red or white in colour with a black dot at the apex, are 6 to 10 mm in diameter. They are **poisonous.**

DID YOU KNOW...

Although the berries are **poisonous,** other parts of the plant have been widely used. The Blackfoot boiled the root and used the resulting infusion as a cold remedy. A mixture of baneberry root and spruce needles was used as a treatment for stomach ailments.

Berries may be red.

Canada anemone

Canada anemone

Anemone canadensis L.

WHERE, WHEN AND WHAT TO LOOK FOR

Canada anemone is a herb that can be found in moist ditches and forested areas, throughout the province. Its white flowers (2.5 to 3 cm across) consist of 5 or 6 sepals (no petals). They bloom from **June to July.** This plant arises from a bulb-like root to a height varying from 20 to 60 cm, depending on the habitat. A whorl of leaves, 4 to 7 cm wide and deeply cleft into 3 to 5 divisions, is located below each flower. The fruit, a dry, brown, single-seeded achene appears in globe-shaped clusters.

SIMILAR SPECIES

A closely related species, long-fruited anemone (*A. cylindrica* A. Gray), grows commonly in open, wooded areas and prairie grassland. The sepals are cream-coloured and have a silky outside.

DID YOU KNOW...

The plains peoples used Canada anemone externally on sores. Anemones contain **caustic irritants** which can be harmful; do not consume, and handle carefully.

long-fruited anemone

prairie crocus, pasque-flower

Anemone patens L.

WHERE, WHEN AND WHAT TO LOOK FOR

The prairie crocus can be commonly found in open jack-pine forests, sand dunes and dry, prairie grassland. **It is one of the earliest-blooming plants in Alberta.** The pale-blue flower has 5 to 7 petal-like sepals, but no petals. Sepals are 2 to 4 cm in length with silky hair on the outer surfaces. The feathery styles have elongated by the time the plant's furry greyish green leaves have fully emerged, so seeds are easily spread by the wind.

DID YOU KNOW...

Native lore refers to the prairie crocus as the 'ears of the earth,' because it seems to spring through the snow to listen for the approach of summer. Native legends also tell of the Great Spirit giving this delicate plant a fur coat to keep it warm through cold spring nights. In fact, the hairs discourage insects and grazing animals. The Blackfoot used the plant for healing, making a poultice from the leaves to ease rheumatic pain. Early European settlers made a dye from the pale-blue sepals and used it to colour Easter eggs.

blue columbine

Aquilegia brevistyla Hook.

WHERE, WHEN AND WHAT TO LOOK FOR

Blue columbine, common to moist aspen and spruce forests, is found in the North Saskatchewan River valley. Nodding or erect flowers (1.5 to 2.5 cm long) bloom from **June through July.** They are composed of 5 blue or purple sepals and 5 yellowish white petals. Basal compound leaves, up to 20 cm long, have 3 leaflets. Stem leaves have 3 lobes. The stem, often hairy above, can grow to a height ranging from 20 to 80 cm. Fruit take the form of pods, 2 cm long, appearing in groups of 5.

DID YOU KNOW...

Native people mashed the ripe seeds and rubbed them into their hair to kill head lice. The leaves provided the base for a lotion to treat sore mouths and throats. In European traditions, seeds taken with wine and saffron were used to treat jaundice and liver obstructions. The young leaves were eaten as a cooked vegetable. A tea made from boiled roots was taken to treat diarrhea.

marsh marigold, cowslip

Caltha palustris L.

WHERE, WHEN AND WHAT TO LOOK FOR

Marsh marigold, or cowslip, grows along stream edges, roadside ditches and shallow ponds. In the Edmonton region, it is found at Wagner Natural Area and Elk Island National Park. It is also common throughout Central Alberta. The flower appears from **May through June** as a yellow bloom (2 to 4 cm across) with 5 to 9 sepals and no petals. The hollow stem grows up to 50 cm tall with kidney-shaped, somewhat fleshy leaves 4 cm in diameter. Basal leaves are long-petioled and stem leaves appear without stalks. Fruit appears as a cluster of 'pods' that open along a seam to release seeds.

DID YOU KNOW...

The pungent leaves of marsh marigold contain a **poison** called 'helleborine.' This **toxin** can be destroyed by boiling the leaves in three changes of water. Unopened buds boiled in the same manner make an excellent pickle. This vegetable was eaten by some as a remedy for coughs and colds. A few drops of the corrosive sap applied daily to a wart will remove it. Some native peoples used marsh marigold as an insecticide.

purple clematis

Clematis occidentalis

(Hornem.) DC.

WHERE, WHEN AND WHAT TO LOOK FOR

The purple clematis is common in open aspen forests on north-facing slopes of the North Saskatchewan River valley. It is a **twisting, semi-woody vine** that grasps onto surrounding vegetation. In **May to late June,** single flowers with 4 to 6 blue sepals (1 to 6 cm long) and no petals appear on long stalks. After the flower fades, styles lengthen to form a dense head of feathery seeds that are easily spread by the wind. Leaves are composed of 3 leaflets, each 2 to 8 cm long. The vine can grow as long as 2 m.

SIMILAR SPECIES

A closely related species, yellow clematis (*C. tangutica* (Max.) Korsh.), prefers sunny open areas along fence lines and edges of forests. It has yellow flowers and 5 leaflets and resembles a yellow Chinese lantern, its other common name.

DID YOU KNOW...

Protoam, a **poisonous** agent that causes respiratory paralysis, is found in purple clematis. This chemical is also found in other species of the Buttercup Family.

veiny meadow rue
Thalictrum venulosum Trel.

female flowers

WHERE, WHEN AND WHAT TO LOOK FOR

Veiny meadow rue is common in aspen forests and moist prairies throughout the province. **Male and female flowers borne on separate plants bloom from June through July.** The male flower (6 to 10 mm long) consists of several yellow stamens. The female flower (6 to 8 mm long) has many green to pinkish purple pistils. Both flowers have 4 to 5 greenish white sepals that fall off soon after blooming. The plant grows from 15 to 90 cm tall It has yellow roots and alternate, compound leaves with 3 to 5 3-lobed leaflets. The leaflets, 2 to 3 cm across, have pale undersides with dark veins. The fruit appears as a cluster of ribbed achenes, 3 to 6.5 mm long.

SIMILAR SPECIES

Two other species of meadow rue (*T. dasycarpum* Fisch. & Ave-Lall. and *T. sparsiflorum* Turcz.) can be found in Edmonton and Central Alberta. Tall meadow rue (*T. dasycarpum*), a more robust plant, has longer leaflets and is found in wet meadows. Flat-fruited meadow rue (*T. sparsiflorum*) has flowers that have stamens and pistils together, making it easy to distinguish.

DID YOU KNOW...

The Blackfoot used the whole plant as a source of perfume.

male flowers

cow parsnip
Heracleum lanatum Michx.

WHERE, WHEN AND WHAT TO LOOK FOR

Cow parsnip is common in moist forests and open meadows throughout the province. White flowers (up to 6 mm across) bloom in umbels up to 30 cm across, from **June to August.** Petals are of varying sizes; the largest flowers appear on the edge of the umbel. Alternate leaves grow up to 30 cm wide and are composed of 3 leaflets which are lobed and prominently veined. The hollow hairy stem grows up to 2.5 m tall. The fruit is small (up to 1 cm long), dry, and flattened with visible lines on its sides.

DID YOU KNOW ...

Cow parsnip belongs to the carrot family, as do caraway and dill. Young roots of cow parsnip can be cooked like parsnips. Seeds add seasoning to soups and stews. The peeled leaf stalk can be eaten fresh, but **take care,** because the peel contains a chemical that can blister skin. A drink made from the roots or seeds was sometimes taken to relieve asthma, colic, colds and cramps.

water parsnip

Sium suave Walt.

WHERE, WHEN AND WHAT TO LOOK FOR

Water parsnip, common along lakeshores and edges of sloughs, is often found growing together with a closely related and poisonous species, water hemlock (*Cicuta maculata* L.). Both species are found throughout Alberta. The small (2 mm across), white flower blooms in umbrella-shaped clusters from **July to September.** The sepals of water parsnip are small or absent; they are triangular and well-developed in water hemlock. The hollow stem of water parsnip grows up to 1 m tall and bears few branches. Its alternate compound leaves have 5 or more narrow leaflets 5 to 10 cm long with serrated edges. The fruit is dry, oval and 2 to 3 mm long, and it has conspicuous ridges. Water hemlock has twice pinnately compound leaves that are longer and wider than those of water parsnip.

SIMILAR SPECIES

Extreme caution should be exercised when collecting water parsnip because it resembles water hemlock, the most poisonous plant in Alberta. The roots of water parsnip can be roasted, fried or eaten raw, but consuming even a small portion of the water hemlock root can be fatal. The **poison** in water hemlock, cicutoxin, causes paralysis of the respiratory muscles and death by asphyxiation. See the comparative descriptions above.

DID YOU KNOW...

The Blackfoot used the Hemlock root as an external poultice and to extract poison from rattlesnake bites.

cattail
Typha latifolia L.

WHERE, WHEN AND WHAT TO LOOK FOR

The cattail, a common marsh plant found along ditches and most margins of sloughs and lakes throughout Alberta, is frequently overlooked as one of North America's edible wild plants. It has 2 types of flowers, male and female, both lacking petals and sepals. The male flowers are borne in a greenish brown terminal spike that is 8 to 15 cm long and about 2 cm in diameter. The female flowers are borne in a brown spike 4 to 5 cm in diameter that is located directly below the male spike. Several basal leaves, each 1 to 3 cm wide and up to 50 cm long, arise from the large, creeping root system. By mid-August, the female spike contains thousands of tiny seeds covered with white hair.

DID YOU KNOW...

Young female cattail flowers can be boiled and eaten like corn on the cob. Male flowers can be dried, ground and used to extend equal amounts of flour in baking. Roots can be boiled and used as a low-fat and equal-protein substitute for rice, corn and potatoes. The Blackfoot applied cattail fluff as an antiseptic to burns and scalds. The Cree chopped and ate the stems to remedy diarrhea. The spongy, olive-green leaves can be woven into baskets and mats. Fluff from the female spikes can be gathered in the fall and used to stuff pillows or as insulating material. It was used extensively to stuff lifejackets during World War I.

common gooseberry

Ribes oxyacanthoides L.

WHERE, WHEN AND WHAT TO LOOK FOR

Look for the common gooseberry in moist areas of aspen and balsam-poplar forests, and occasionally in white-spruce stands. It is found throughout Alberta. Clusters of flowers appear in leaf axils from **May through June.** Flowers (4 to 5 mm long) are composed of 5 greenish white sepals (curved backwards) and 5 white or greenish white, petals. The shrub grows up to 2 m tall. Many prickles cluster at the base of its alternate leaves. Leaves are maple-leaf-shaped, 3-lobed and 3 to 5 cm across. Branches become less prickly as they mature. Gooseberry fruit matures to reddish purple and measures 10 to 15 mm in diameter.

DID YOU KNOW...

The Blood people ate the boiled leaves with sugar. An extract from the roots deodorizes hair, smelly feet and general body odour. The gooseberry fruit contains citric acid and pectin, making it a good choice for jelly.

wild red currant

Ribes triste Pall.

WHERE, WHEN AND WHAT TO LOOK FOR

Moist areas of aspen-balsam and mixed-wood forests are the habitat of the wild red currant. It is found in Northern and Central Alberta. Greenish pink to purplish red flowers (5 mm across) bloom from **May through June.** They appear at the same time as the leaves, in numbers of 6 to 20, drooping in clusters 5 to 10 cm in length. The shrub can grow to a height of 1 m and, happily for berry-pickers, has no prickles. Alternate leaves are maple-leaf-shaped with 3 to 5 coarsely serrated lobes 5 to 10 cm across. The bright-red berries are about 4 mm in diameter. Edible but tart, they are ready for picking in July.

DID YOU KNOW...

A tea made from the leaves was once a general medicine for women's ailments. An infusion of the peeled stems can be used as an eyewash. Currants have a high pectin content and make excellent jellies and syrups.

spreading dogbane

Apocynum androsaemifolium L.

WHERE, WHEN AND WHAT TO LOOK FOR

Spreading dogbane is common in habitats ranging from dry, sandy areas to open forests. Fragrant, pinkish white flowers (6 mm long) bloom from **June through August.** The bell-shaped corolla has dark pink lines on the inside and is formed by the union of 5 petals. Flowers are borne at the ends of reddish green stems that contain a milky-white juice. Stems can grow to a height of 1 m but are more common at 50 cm. Bright-green opposite leaves, 2.5 to 7.5 cm in length, turn golden yellow to red in the autumn. **Poisonous fruit** form in late July as pairs of reddish green pods, 2 to 10 cm long. Other parts of the plant may also be **poisonous**: do not consume.

DID YOU KNOW ...

Because of dogbane's high latex content, several attempts have been made to grow the plant commercially for the production of rubber. The similar appearance of the latex to milk led to the native tradition of using a decoction of dogbane applied to a mother's breasts to increase lactation. The Blackfoot also used the milky juice as a shampoo to make hair shiny.

bunchberry, pigeonberry

Cornus canadensis L.

WHERE, WHEN AND WHAT TO LOOK FOR

Bunchberry, or pigeonberry, is common to most wooded areas in Alberta. A delicate herb that has been grown in English gardens for over two centuries, it likes cool shady areas, especially under evergreens where the soil is quite acidic. Its 'large white flower' appears in June and is actually a cluster of 5 to 15 small flowers surrounded by 4 white bracts that serve to attract insects. Below the 'flower' grows a whorl of 4 to 6 oval-shaped leaves, each about 8 cm in length. Two smaller, opposite leaves appear on the stem below the whorled leaves. In August, small, red, edible berries form that are tasteless to humans but readily eaten by grouse and other birds.

DID YOU KNOW ...

The Cree call bunchberry *kawiscowimin*, meaning 'itchy chin berry,' a reference to the rough surface of the leaves.

red-osier dogwood

Cornus stolonifera Michx.

WHERE, WHEN AND WHAT TO LOOK FOR

Red-osier dogwood is a shrub that inhabits moist riverbanks and wooded areas throughout Alberta. It grows to heights of up to 3 m. **It can be easily identified in any season by its bright-red bark.** Small (1 mm wide), white flowers, 8 to 12 in number, appear from **June through August** in flat-topped clusters, 3 to 6 cm wide. Opposite leaves, 3 to 8 cm long, are dark-green on the top and lighter-green underneath; they turn reddish purple in fall. Lower branches sometimes root and form new plants. The white, sometimes tinged with purple, juicy berry, is 2 to 3 mm in diameter. It is **inedible** because it is very bitter.

DID YOU KNOW…

The Cree and Blackfoot used the bark and leaves of red-osier dogwood as an additive to tobacco. Native peoples from northern Alberta used the outer bark to make a dye and a tanning solution for hides. Snow blindness was treated with an eyewash made from the white berries. Stems of red-osier dogwood were woven into birch baskets to add colour.

lesser duckweed

large duckweed

Spirodela polyrhiza (L.) Schleiden

WHERE, WHEN AND WHAT TO LOOK FOR

Large duckweed is common along lakeshores and sloughs in the Central Alberta. It can be found, for example, at Clifford E. Lee Bird Sanctuary and Elk Island National Park. **Its flowers are very rarely seen because of their small size and lack of petals or sepals.** Male flowers have a single stamen, female flowers have a single pistil. Large duckweed is a small, green, free-floating plant, 3 to 8 mm wide, with several small rootlets attached to its reddish purple underside. The species name, polyrhiza, means 'many roots.'

SIMILAR SPECIES

A closely related species, lesser duckweed (*Lemna minor* L.), has a green underside with a single root. It is quite common in still waters of the aspen parkland. It is also found at Clifford E. Lee Bird Sanctuary and Elk Island National Park.

DID YOU KNOW...

Duckweed reproduces by budding, which means that new plants form on the edge of the parent thallus (the plant body). Buds increase in number to form extensive colonies. In the fall, duckweed produces buds on the edge of the thallus. These buds overwinter on the bottom of ponds and, in the spring, rise to the surface to form new colonies.

large duckweed

35

fireweed, tall willowherb

Epilobium angustifolium L.

WHERE, WHEN AND WHAT TO LOOK FOR

Fireweed is found in large colonies in open forests, along river-banks and in forest-burn areas. It grows to a height of 3 m and was given the common name 'fireweed' because it is one of the first plants to appear after a forest fire. Pink to light-purple flowers (2 to 3 cm across) appear in terminal clusters and bloom from **June through August.** Alternate leaves have smooth edges and are 5 to 20 cm long and up to 3.5 cm wide. The fruit, a pinkish green capsule or pod, is often 4-angled and 4 to 10 cm long. Pods contain many seeds, each with tufts of white hair, 9 to 14 cm long.

DID YOU KNOW...

Young shoots of fireweed make an excellent vegetable that tastes like asparagus. The whole plant is readily eaten by live-stock. Flowers are a good source of nectar for bees. The roots and leaves have been used as a remedy for diarrhea, eczema and sore throats.

ostrich fern

Matteuccia struthiopteris

(L.) Todaro

WHERE, WHEN AND WHAT TO LOOK FOR

Ostrich fern inhabits the moist woods along the North
Saskatchewan River in southwest Edmonton and the Lesser
Slave Lake and Athabasca regions. It grows to a height of 1.5 m
and is recognized by its 4 to 6 light-green basal leaves (fronds)
that arise from a stout rhizome (underground stem) and are
pinnately divided. As with all ferns, true flowers (sepals, petals
and seeds) are absent and ostrich fern reproduces by spores.
Spores are borne on short, stiff, fertile fronds 20 to 60 cm long
that are olive-green when young and dark brown at maturity.

DID YOU KNOW …

Leaves of this plant resemble ostrich feathers—hence the name
'ostrich fern.' Young leaves, or fiddleheads, are edible and are
high in iron and Vitamins A, B and C. Rhizomes have been used
in pastries and beer-making. The lower part of the sterile frond
was eaten to relieve back pain.

toadflax, butter-and-eggs

Linaria vulgaris Hill.

toadflax

WHERE, WHEN AND WHAT TO LOOK FOR

Toadflax, or butter-and-eggs, was introduced to our region from Europe as a garden flower. Now classified as a **noxious weed,** it is common on roadsides, railway grades, ditches and waste areas. The orange-throated, yellow flower (2 to 3 cm long) has a spur approximately 1 cm long at its base. It grows to heights of up to 60 cm, with alternate leaves up to 7.5 cm long and less than 1 cm wide. The extensive, creeping rootstock allows it to thrive.

SIMILAR SPECIES

A related species, common red Indian paintbrush (*Castilleja miniata* Dougl.), has green flowers and red to pink bracts that are often mistaken for petals. It is found throughout Central Alberta.

DID YOU KNOW ...

The common name 'toadflax' originated in England. 'Toad' meant worthless and 'flax' suggested that the leaves resembled those of the Flax Family *(Linaceae).* Toadflax spreads by an underground rhizome making it hard to eradicate in cropland.

common red Indian paintbrush

wild blue flax

Linum lewisii Pursh

WHERE, WHEN AND WHAT TO LOOK FOR

A plant commonly found growing in dry prairie grassland and on south-facing slopes, wild blue flax can be seen in the North Saskatchewan River valley. Its pale-blue flowers (1.5 to 3 cm across) appear from **June through August** and have dark-blue lines radiating from their centres. Petals do not survive more than one day. The plant rises from a woody rootstock to heights of up to 60 cm. Alternate leaves are 1 to 2 cm long, narrow and numerous. The fruit is a dry capsule, 5 mm in diameter, containing 8 to 10 seeds.

DID YOU KNOW...

The species name *lewisii* comes from the American explorer, Captain Meriwether Lewis, who discovered wild blue flax. The stem fibres have been used as a substitute for string. The seeds are quite nutritious and contain linseed oil. Early settlers made a poultice of powdered seeds, cornmeal and boiling water. This paste was applied to infected wounds.

white geranium

Geranium richardsonii

Fisch. & Trautv.

WHERE, WHEN AND WHAT TO LOOK FOR

The white geranium inhabits edges of aspen and spruce forests in Central Alberta. White flowers (up to 3 cm wide) composed of 5 petals with 5 to 9 distinct pinkish purple veins per petal bloom from **June through July.** Numerous bright-green opposite leaves, 3 to 15 cm in diameter, have 3 to 7 coarsely-serrated lobes. The fruit, a dry capsule with a long beak, splits into 5 parts and releases 5 distinctly-veined seeds.

SIMILAR SPECIES

A closely related species, Bicknell's geranium (*G. bicknellii* Britt.), is common in waste areas and roadsides. Petals are pink and less than 1 cm long. The leaves are 5 lobed.

DID YOU KNOW...

The leaves of the white geranium are edible and can be added to soups and salads. A bath made with geranium leaves is said to stimulate the skin.

wild sarsaparilla

Aralia nudicaulis L.

WHERE, WHEN AND WHAT TO LOOK FOR

Wild sarsaparilla is a common herbaceous plant of aspen and mixed-wood forests. It is found throughout our area. Twenty to 40 greenish white flowers (each 3 mm across) emerge in globe-shaped clusters called 'umbels' and bloom from **June through July.** Usually 3 (but anywhere from 2 to 7) of these umbels arise on a single stem from an extensive, creeping rootstock. The compound leaf reaches a height of up to 60 cm. The compound basal leaf has 3 divisions each with 3 to 5 minutely serrated leaflets. Clusters of purplish black berries, 4 to 6 mm in diameter, ripen in August.

DID YOU KNOW...

Wild sarsaparilla, an ingredient of the original root beer, has medicinal properties. The roots, sometimes up to 1 m long, have been collected and eaten fresh to treat chills, fevers and rheumatism. The aromatic roots make an excellent tea. The fruit is edible, but tasteless.

41

grass-of-Parnassus
Parnassia palustris L.

WHERE, WHEN AND WHAT TO LOOK FOR

Grass-of-Parnassus inhabits wet areas in ditches, bogs and shady woods throughout Alberta. Five greenish yellow, sterile stamens called 'staminodes' make this one of the prettiest flowers in Alberta. The flowers (2.5 cm wide) bloom from **June through September** and are composed of 5 green sepals and 5 white petals with distinct, green veins. The plant grows up to 35 cm tall with 1 or more flowering stems. Basal leaves have smooth edges. They are heart-shaped and 1 to 2.5 cm wide. A single stem leaf, located near the midpoint of the flowering stem, makes grass-of-Parnassus easy to identify. The fruit is a dry capsule up to 1 cm long, containing many brown seeds.

SIMILAR SPECIES

Three other species are found in the mountains and foothills of Alberta. Each species has 1 stem leaf. Fringed grass-of-Parnassus (*P. fimbriata* Konig) found in moist springy areas has frilled petals with 5 distinct veins. Alpine grass-of-Parnassus (*P. kotzebuei* Cham. & Schlecht) is found in moist alpine slopes and has 3 veins per petal. Small flowered grass-of-Parnassus (*P. parviflora* DC.) is found in boggy areas and has 5 to 7 distinct veins per petal.

harebell
Campanula rotundifolia L.

WHERE, WHEN AND WHAT TO LOOK FOR

Harebell grows on dry hillsides, meadows and the edges of open woods. It grows up to 45 cm tall and is found throughout Alberta. Blue, bell-shaped flowers (1.5 to 2.5 cm long) bloom from **June through August.** Flowering stems, each bearing 1 to 5 flowers, arise from the rootstock. Basal leaves are oval; alternate stem leaves are narrow and 1 to 7.5 cm long. The fruit is a papery capsule containing many seeds.

SIMILAR SPECIES

A closely related species, garden harebell (*C. rapunculoides* L.), has larger flowers and can be found in waste areas where it has escaped from cultivation.

DID YOU KNOW...

The Cree chopped the dried root and made it into a compress to stop bleeding, reduce swelling and assist in healing. They also chewed the root to relieve heart ailments.

bog rosemary

Andromeda polifolia L.

WHERE, WHEN AND WHAT TO LOOK FOR

Bog rosemary is a small shrub that inhabits peat bogs and swamps of the boreal forest. The urn-shaped flowers (6 to 10 mm long) bloom from **May through June** and are composed of 5 pinkish white sepals and 5 pink petals. The shrub grows up to only 40 cm. It has weak branches bearing alternate leaves 2 to 5 cm long and 5 mm wide. The upper leaf surface is dark green and the leaf margin is rolled toward the white underside. Fruit appears as a dry, pinkish purple capsule, 8 mm in diameter, containing numerous seeds.

DID YOU KNOW...

The leaves and stems of bog rosemary contain a **toxin** which lowers blood pressure and causes shortness of breath.

bearberry, kinnickinnick

Arctostaphylos uva-ursi (L.) Spreng.

WHERE, WHEN AND WHAT TO LOOK FOR

Although usually associated with pine forests, bearberry is a low-trailing shrub that can also be found in dry sandhills. A pinkish white, urn-shaped flower (about 5 mm long) appears from **May through July.** Leathery, thick, alternate leaves (1.5 to 2 cm long) remain green for several seasons. A network of veins on the leaf underside easily distinguishes this plant from the bog cranberry *(see page 49)*, the underside of which is dotted. A bright-red berry, 6 to 10 mm in diameter, appears in August and often remains until the following summer. The dry, tasteless berry contains 5 nutlets.

DID YOU KNOW...

The Vitamin C and carbohydrate content of bearberry make it an important survival food. The red fruit remains on the stems throughout the winter, making it accessible to humans and animals. The acidic berries are said to relieve pain associated with kidney stones. Eating too many of them can cause constipation, and they have been used as a treatment for diarrhea. A tea made from the leaves was used as a diuretic and astringent. Early European explorers and trappers dried the leaves and used them as a tobacco substitute.

Labrador tea

Ledum groenlandicum Oeder

WHERE, WHEN AND WHAT TO LOOK FOR

Labrador tea, a common shrub of bogs and moist coniferous forests in Northern Canada, grows abundantly in Northern and Central Alberta. Clusters of 5 to 20 small, white flowers (about 6 mm wide) appear in **late June to early July,** and produce dry, inedible fruits in August. Straggling stems of Labrador tea grow to a height of 1.2 metres and are coated with brown, velvety hairs. Alternate leaves, 1 to 5 cm in length, are green year-'round, and have a woolly, rust-coloured underside. An amateur botanist will need to look closely to identify this unusual feature, because the leaf margins roll down and toward the centre.

DID YOU KNOW...

Natives and European explorers made a tea from the leaves and flowers of this plant as a remedy for coughs and colds. Caution must be used in preparing this tea, because leaves boiled for longer than ten minutes release a **toxin** that can produce headaches, cramps and paralysis. Leaves release a fragrance when crushed and can be added to pot-pourris.

small bog cranberry, swamp cranberry

Oxycoccus microcarpus Turcz.

WHERE, WHEN AND WHAT TO LOOK FOR

Small bog cranberry or swamp cranberry is a common but inconspicuous plant that grows on moss in cool, wet bogs. A delicate, trailing evergreen, it reaches lengths varying from 10 to 40 cm. **Look for it at Wagner Natural Area.** Its nodding flowers bloom from **June through July** and are composed of 4 green sepals and 4 pinkish petals (5 to 8 mm long) that curve backwards. Alternate, evergreen leaves are 3 to 8 mm long, with margins that roll over to an underside that is light green to white. Edible fruit appears as a reddish coloured, speckled berry, 5 to 14 mm in diameter.

DID YOU KNOW...

The fruit of small bog cranberry is tart and acidic, and can be enjoyed fresh, dried or frozen. Some native peoples stewed the berries and served them with smoked fish. Some people recommend eating cranberry pulp to prevent asthma attacks. Berries provide a red dye.

blueberry

Vaccinium myrtilloides Michx.

WHERE, WHEN AND WHAT TO LOOK FOR

A low shrub up to 40 cm tall, the blueberry grows in dry sandy woods. It can usually be found growing in jack-pine forests. Clusters of 2 to 10 flowers, each a union of 5 greenish white to pinkish white petals (4 to 6 mm long), bloom from **June through July.** Twigs have short hairs. Alternate leaves are 1 to 4 cm long and are also covered with short, soft hairs. An edible, blue berry, 4 to 7 mm in diameter, usually ripens by mid-August.

DID YOU KNOW...

This easily recognized fruit is popular with humans and wildlife. Jams, jellies and pies usually come to mind when one thinks of blueberries, but this small shrub has many other uses. A fragrant, diuretic tea can be made from the berries that is said to be a blood tonic. A tea can also be made from the leaves, but it is bitter. Some native peoples used the berries to dye porcupine quills.

bog cranberry
Vaccinium vitis-idaea L.

WHERE, WHEN AND WHAT TO LOOK FOR

Bog cranberry inhabits dry, open coniferous forests and dry areas in bogs and muskegs. A low, trailing shrub that seldom grows over 10 cm tall and 30 cm long, it is found throughout our region. Pink-to-white flowers bloom from **June through July.** They are composed of 4 united petals (6 mm long) appearing in terminal clusters. Alternate leaves, 1 cm long, remain green year-round. They appear dark green on top and light green with many small dots on the underside. A bright-red, juicy berry, 5 to 10 mm across, ripens in mid-August.

DID YOU KNOW...

Some say that drinking a juice made from the berries cleanses the urinary tract. The fruit is high in Vitamin C and was gathered as a winter food source. The tart berries freeze well and can be added to pancakes, muffins and breads.

49

twinflower

Linnaea borealis L.

WHERE, WHEN AND WHAT TO LOOK FOR

Twinflower grows in leaf litter and moss. A semi-woody plant, its trailing stems can reach 1 m in length. Common in aspen and mixed-wood forests, it is often found in Edmonton and Central Alberta. Pinkish white pendant flowers (8 to 15 mm long) bloom from **June through July.** The fragrant blooms are funnel-shaped and appear in pairs on a stalk about 10 cm tall. Evergreen leaves are opposite, oval-shaped and 8 to 15 mm across. Each leaf has 2 pairs of notches near the leaf apex. The fruit is a 1-seeded capsule, about 5 mm long.

DID YOU KNOW...

The genus name, *Linnaea*, is named after Carolus Linnaeus, a Swedish botanist. Linnaeus developed the scientific classification system that we still use today.

twining honeysuckle

Lonicera dioica L.

WHERE, WHEN AND WHAT TO LOOK FOR

Twining honeysuckle is a woody vine that climbs on trees, shrubs and fences. It inhabits aspen forests and is found throughout Alberta. Young yellow flowers (1.5 to 2.5 cm long) are found in clusters inside bowl-shaped, united leaves. Blossoms appear from **July through August**, and they turn red as they mature. The vine grows up to 2 m and has shredded bark. Opposite, oval leaves, 5 to 8 cm long, are smooth on top and hairy on the underside. Red berries, 5 to 8 mm in diameter, ripen in August.

DID YOU KNOW...

The hollow branches of twining honeysuckle made good stems for corn-cob pipes. Stems can also serve as drinking straws. An infusion of the inner bark works as a diuretic.

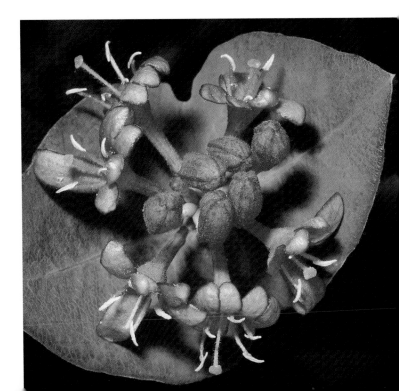

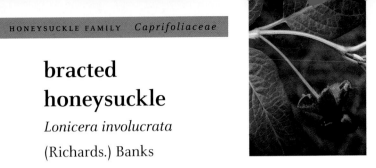

bracted honeysuckle

Lonicera involucrata

(Richards.) Banks

WHERE, WHEN AND WHAT TO LOOK FOR

Bracted honeysuckle grows in moist areas along streams and open meadows. The 1 to 3 m tall shrub can be found in all areas of Central Alberta. Yellow, tube-shaped flowers (1 to 1.5 cm long) appear in **June,** borne in pairs and surrounded by 2 green or purplish green bracts. The shrub has brownish green bark and opposite leaves, 5 to 15 cm long, with prominent veins. Purplish black, shiny berries, 6 to 10 mm in diameter, are partially surrounded by the 2 bracts that turn reddish purple as they mature. **The berries are inedible and possibly poisonous.**

DID YOU KNOW...

Native peoples, early European settlers, miners and hunters consumed the fruit of this plant, despite its risk.

red elder, elderberry

Sambucus racemosa L.

WHERE, WHEN AND WHAT TO LOOK FOR

Red elder, or elderberry, inhabits edges of mixed-wood forests and can be found in the North Saskatchewan River valley in Edmonton, but it is not common in Central Alberta. Yellowish white flowers (3 to 6 mm across) appear from **May through June** in clusters 5 to 10 cm wide. The shrub reaches a height of 3 m, with several stems arising from the rootstock. Opposite compound leaves have 5 to 7 sharply serrated leaflets that are 5 to 17 cm long and 2 to 6 cm wide. Fruit forms as a black or bright-red berry, 5 to 6 mm wide, containing 3 to 5 seeds. The inedible berries ripen in August.

DID YOU KNOW...

The elderberry has many legendary uses, although it is reported to be **poisonous.** Folklore reports that the wood cures toothaches, freckles and colds. When planted around the house, it supposedly keeps the house safe, guarantees a long life, fends off snakes and mosquitoes and prevents warts. A tea made from dried flowers was used to treat coughs and sore throats. Native peoples made pipe stems and musical instruments from the dried branches.

snowberry

Symphoricarpos albus

(L.) Blake

WHERE, WHEN AND WHAT TO LOOK FOR

An inconspicuous shrub growing in moist aspen and spruce forests, snowberry is found throughout Alberta. The delicate branches grow up to 50 cm tall. Bell-shaped, pinkish white flowers (4 to 7 mm long) bloom from **June through July.** They appear in clusters of 2 or 3 and are borne in the upper and terminal leaf axils. Opposite, oval leaves (1 to 4 cm long) have soft hairs on the underside. The fruit—a waxy, white berry—is 6 to 12 mm in diameter.

SIMILAR SPECIES

A closely related species, buckbrush (*S. occidentalis* Hook.) has flowers whose stamens are longer than the petals, unlike those in snowberry *(see page 55).*

DID YOU KNOW...

The juicy, white fruit of snowberry is a strong laxative. The Blackfoot used the plant as a broom.

buckbrush
Symphoricarpos occidentalis
Hook.

WHERE, WHEN AND WHAT TO LOOK FOR

Buckbrush inhabits dry open areas and the edges of aspen forests. In the Edmonton area, it is found on the south-facing slopes of the North Saskatchewan River valley. It is a common shrub in Alberta. Buckbrush grows to 1 m tall and forms extensive colonies. Pinkish white flowers (6 mm long) bloom from **June through July,** appearing in clusters at the ends of stems. Its bark is copper-coloured. Opposite leaves are 2 to 6 cm long, oval-shaped and greyish green. Whitish green berries, 8 to 10 mm in diameter, first appear in August, and turn purple as they mature.

DID YOU KNOW...

Pioneers named this shrub 'water-brush,' because they believed it grew in areas where the water table was close to the surface. The Blackfoot made arrow shafts from stems of the buckbrush.

low-bush cranberry

Viburnum edule (Michx.) Raf.

WHERE, WHEN AND WHAT TO LOOK FOR

Low-bush cranberry is common in moist, heavily wooded forests in our region. Clusters of 3 to 30 white flowers, each about 7 mm wide, bloom from **June through July.** The shrub grows up to 2 m tall and has greyish brown bark. Opposite leaves (6 to 10 cm long) have 3 indistinct lobes and 3 to 5 prominent veins radiating from the leaf base. Bright-red berries, 1 cm in diameter, contain a single seed and appear from August to September. Usually 2 to 5 berries per cluster reach maturity.

DID YOU KNOW ...

The fruit of low-bush cranberry is an excellent source of Vitamin C. The berries are delicious fresh or made into juice or jellies. The tart fruit flavour is improved if the berries are picked after a frost. The Cree made a tea from flower buds, tips of twigs, leaves and stems to relieve sore throats. They also chewed unopened flower buds and applied them to sores on the lips.

high-bush cranberry

Viburnum opulus L.

WHERE, WHEN AND WHAT TO LOOK FOR

High-bush cranberry, a common shrub of aspen forests in the
Edmonton and Red Deer areas, is easily identified by its large,
white flower clusters, up to 15 cm wide. Flower clusters appear
in **June** and contain two types of flowers. The larger, sterile
flowers around the edge attract insect pollinators. The smaller
(about 7 mm across), inner flowers produce the tart, reddish
orange fruit. The shrub has grey bark and can grow to a height
of 4 m. Opposite, dark-green leaves, 6 to 12 cm long and similar
in shape to maple leaves, turn a brilliant reddish purple in the
fall.

DID YOU KNOW ...

European explorers mixed high-bush cranberries with fish eggs,
then dried the mixture and preserved it in moose stomachs to
provide a source of Vitamin C and protein when food was
scarce. Today, the tart fruit is commonly used for jams and
jellies. Cranberries can be used as a tea which is said to relieve
nervousness and cramps, and to make a juice with a strong
diuretic effect, said to help clear up minor bladder infections.

common horsetail, scouring rush

Equisetum arvense L.

reproductive stem

WHERE, WHEN AND WHAT TO LOOK FOR

Common horsetail inhabits moist woods, roadsides, riverbanks and wet meadows throughout Alberta. True flowers (sepals, petals and seeds) are absent. This species has 2 types of stems, each up to 50 cm tall. The brown to pinkish green fertile stems appear in early **May**. These spore producing stems have cone-like structures called 'strobili.' These stems wither soon after 'fruiting.' Green sterile stems appear in **late May** and produce food for the next year's growth. The sterile stems have whorled branches at each node. Leaves are reduced to 8 to 12 brown, tooth-like scales and are located at these nodes.

DID YOU KNOW...

Horsetails, or scouring-rush as they are sometimes called, have a very high silica content. Scouring-rush got its name from the pioneers, who scrubbed their pots and pans with this plant. It also made a good substitute for sandpaper. This plant was once a valuable commodity because it polished arrows and wooden articles. A wash made from this plant reduces offensive perspiration, such as foot odour. Horsetails may be **poisonous** to horses.

vegetative stem

blue-eyed grass

Sisyrinchium montanum Greene

WHERE, WHEN AND WHAT TO LOOK FOR

Blue-eyed grass, a common plant, inhabits moist open areas. Flowers (1 cm long), composed of 3 blue sepals and 3 blue petals, bloom from **June through July.** Because this plant resembles grass, it is often overlooked when not in flower. It grows up to 30 cm tall, with grass-like basal leaves, 3 mm wide and 2 to 6 cm long, that are set edgewise on the stem. The fruit is a dry, globe-shaped capsule containing numerous small, black seeds which can be quickly dispersed by wind.

SIMILAR SPECIES

A closely related species, mountain blue-eyed grass (*S. septentrionale* Bicknell), has narrower leaves and pale, bluish white flowers. It is found in the foothills of Alberta.

DID YOU KNOW...

The seeds of blue-eyed grass are easily germinated in moist, sandy soil.

nodding onion
Allium cernuum Roth

WHERE, WHEN AND WHAT TO LOOK FOR

Nodding onion can be found in the North Saskatchewan River valley and Clifford E. Lee Bird Sanctuary. This plant inhabits prairie slopes and open aspen forests, arising from a slender bulb to a height of about 40 cm. Its nodding, pinkish white flowers (4 to 6 mm long) bloom from **June through July** in clusters of 10 to 20. Each flower consists of 3 sepals and 3 petals, all similar in appearance. Numerous basal leaves grow up to 30 cm long. Leaves have the distinct odour of onion and are edible. Fruit appears as a dry capsule with 3 to 6 small black seeds.

DID YOU KNOW...

All parts of the wild onion are edible and are said to have medicinal properties. Wild onion has been used to add flavour to wild game and to aid in digestion. Herbalists prescribe onions for colds, earaches and as an antiseptic for wounds. Nodding onion is a valuable food source for ground squirrels.

fairy-bells
Disporum trachycarpum
(S. Wats.) B.&H.

WHERE, WHEN AND WHAT TO LOOK FOR

Fairy-bells grow in moist aspen forests, often alongside wild sarsaparilla and baneberry. It is common throughout Alberta. Greenish yellow flowers (1 to 2 cm long) bloom from **May through June.** Flowers are composed of 3 sepals and 3 petals, all similar in appearance, growing in groups of 1 to 4 at the end of stems. The plant grows to a height of about 60 cm. It has drooping branches and dark-green, parallel-veined alternate leaves up to 7.5 cm long and 5 cm wide. A deep-red berry, 1 cm in diameter with a velvety surface, appears from July through August and contain 4 to 18 seeds.

DID YOU KNOW ...

The velvety fruit of fairy-bells can be eaten raw and has a distinct apricot flavour. The Blackfoot call this plant *im-a-toch-kot*, which means 'dog feet.'

western wood lily

Lilium philadelphicum L.

WHERE, WHEN AND WHAT TO LOOK FOR

The western wood lily, floral emblem of Saskatchewan, is occasionally found in Central Alberta along roadsides and edges of aspen groves. Once quite common, its numbers have been greatly reduced by picking, and by agricultural expansion. Large, showy reddish orange flowers are composed of 3 sepals and 3 petals, all similar in appearance. Below the flower grows a whorl of 4 to 8 leaves much like the alternate stem leaves, all up to 8 cm in length.

DID YOU KNOW...

Many natives crushed the leaves of the western wood lily to make a poultice for the bite of a small poisonous spider, although we no longer know exactly which species. The Cree ate the bulbs and seeds of this plant.

wild lily-of-the-valley
Maianthemum canadense Desf.

WHERE, WHEN AND WHAT TO LOOK FOR

Wild lily-of-the-valley can be found growing in moss or leaf litter in moist aspen and spruce forests. Look for it throughout Northern and Central Alberta. A white flower (4 to 6 mm wide) blooms in **June** in dense, terminal clusters. Each flower consists of 2 sepals and 2 petals, similar in size and colour. The plant arises from a slender branching rhizome to a height of 15 cm, with 1 to 3 alternate leaves that are up to 8 cm long and parallel-veined. The fruit is a speckled, red berry, 3 to 4 mm in diameter.

SIMILAR SPECIES

Cultivated lily-of-the-valley (*Convallaria majus* L.), commonly found in gardens, originated in Europe. It has 3 sepals and 3 petals, unlike the wild species which has 2 sepals and 2 petals, and may be **toxic** if eaten.

DID YOU KNOW...

The berries of wild lily-of-the-valley should not be eaten in large quantities since they cause indigestion and may actually be **poisonous**.

star-flowered Solomon's-seal

Smilacina stellata (L.) Desf.

WHERE, WHEN AND WHAT TO LOOK FOR

Star-flowered Solomon's-seal, a herb found in moist areas of meadows and open forests, is common throughout our region. A white flower (6 to 10 mm across) blooms in **June,** appearing in terminal clusters of 5 to 12. Each flower is composed of 3 sepals and 3 petals, all similar in appearance. The stem grows to a height of 70 cm and appears bent. Its 6 to 12 light green leaves (2 to 10 cm long) are alternate, although they appear to be opposite unless you look closely. A purplish green berry with 6 stripes appears from July through August.

SIMILAR SPECIES

A closely related species, three-leaved Solomon's-seal (*S. trifolia* (L.) Desf.), has 3 leaves and can be found growing in bogs and marshes. It is found throughout Northern and Central Alberta.

DID YOU KNOW...

The slender roots were gathered and dried in the fall to be ground into a powder that could be applied to wounds to stop bleeding. Livestock readily eat star-flowered Solomon's-seal.

bedstraw
Galium boreale L.

WHERE, WHEN AND WHAT TO LOOK FOR

Bedstraw is a common plant in Alberta. It grows in open meadows and on the edges of aspen forests. Fragrant, 4-lobed, white flowers (3 mm across) appear in dense clusters from **June through July.** Square stems grow to a height of 80 cm. Whorled leaves, 2 to 5 cm long with 3 prominent veins, appear in groups of 4. Fruit takes the form of nutlets, 1 mm in diameter, borne in pairs and covered with dense white hairs.

DID YOU KNOW...

The common name, 'bedstraw,' originates from the plant being used as a mattress stuffing by European settlers. The Cree made a red dye to colour porcupine quills by boiling the roots. Boiled for a longer period of time, the root produced a yellow dye. Bedstraw belongs to the same family as coffee, and the flavour and aroma of its seeds are said to make it the best coffee substitute of any plant in Canada.

wild mint

Mentha arvensis L.

WHERE, WHEN AND WHAT TO LOOK FOR

Wild mint grows along the margins of sloughs and in wet
marshy areas. It can be found throughout Alberta. Purplish blue,
tube-shaped flowers (3 mm long) appear clustered in the leaf
axils from **June through August.** Stamens are longer than the 4
or 5-lobed corolla. Greenish purple, square stems grow to 50 cm
tall. Opposite leaves, 1 to 4 cm long and 1 to 1.5 cm wide, have
the characteristic mint fragrance when crushed. The fruit
appears as 4 nutlets enclosed by the sepals.

DID YOU KNOW ...

This plant can be easily recognized by its distinctive scent. A
delicious tea can be made from fresh or dried leaves and stems
and has been used to treat colds. The Blackfoot used the leaves
to flavour meat or pemmican. They also boiled snares and traps
with the leaves to mask human scent.

marsh hedge nettle

skullcap
Scutellaria galericulata L.

WHERE, WHEN AND WHAT TO LOOK FOR

Wet meadows and the edges of sloughs are the places to find skullcap. It is a common marsh plant in Edmonton and Central Alberta. Blue-to-purple flowers (1 to 2 cm long) appear singly or in pairs in each leaf axil. The square stems arise from creeping rootstocks to a length of about 80 cm. Opposite leaves are 2.5 to 7 cm long with wavy margins. The fruit grows as 4 nutlets surrounded by sepals.

SIMILAR SPECIES

A related species, marsh hedge nettle (*Stachys palustris* L.), has flowers up to 1 cm long that range from pale purple to white with purple spots. Its opposite leaves are light green and densely hairy. The tuberous root of this plant can be eaten boiled or dried.

DID YOU KNOW...

Although skullcap is edible and not considered poisonous, it should not be eaten in large quantities because it may cause wakefulness and excitability.

skullcap

dwarf mistletoe

Arceuthobium americanum Nutt.

witches' broom on pine

WHERE, WHEN AND WHAT TO LOOK FOR

Dwarf mistletoe can be seen growing as a parasite on the branches and trunks of pines at Redwater sandhills and east Central Alberta. Pines infected with this parasite can be easily recognized because they produce dense clumps of branches called 'witches' brooms.' Two types of greenish yellow flowers appear in **early May.** Male flowers have a 3-part calyx and 3 stamens; female flowers have a 2-part calyx and 1 pistil. The fragile stem, also greenish yellow, grows from 2 to 10 cm in length and bears many branches. Opposite leaves are very small, scale-like and fused to the stem. The fruit is a 1-seeded capsule about 3 mm long. When mature, the fruit explodes, dispersing a seed with a sticky pulp. This pulp enables the seed to attach itself to pine branches where it germinates. Seeds can also be transported to other pines by birds and squirrels.

SIMILAR SPECIES

A related species, Christmas mistletoe (*Phoradendron flavescens* (Pursh.) Nutt.), is commonly sold at Christmas time. The genus name is Greek for 'thief' and 'tree,' referring to the parasitic nature of this plant.

male flowers

wild buckwheat

wild morning glory
Convolvulus sepium L.

WHERE, WHEN AND WHAT TO LOOK FOR

Wild morning glory climbs on shrubs and trees along forest edges. It blooms in June at Government House Park in Edmonton in the North Saskatchewan River valley. Its funnel-shaped flower (3 to 6 cm across) is a combination of 5 green sepals enclosed by 2 large bracts and 5 white to pink-tinged, petals borne in leaf axils. The vine grows to several metres long with alternate, triangular leaves, 5 to 13 cm long. The fruit appears as a dry capsule with 4 black seeds that may remain dormant for many years until conditions favour germination.

SIMILAR SPECIES

A closely related species, field bindweed (*C. arvensis* L.), has pinkish white flowers (3 to 5 mm long) and smaller leaves 2 to 4 cm long. It is often confused with wild buckwheat (*Polygonum convolvulus* L.), a member of the Buckwheat Family. The flowers of wild buckwheat are 2–4 mm wide. Both weeds, introduced from Europe or Asia, are difficult to eradicate from cultivated fields.

DID YOU KNOW...

Both wild morning glory and field bindweed contain a bitter, milky juice that causes **nausea** if eaten.

wild morning glory

peppergrass

Lepidium densiflorum Schrad.

WHERE, WHEN AND WHAT TO LOOK FOR

Peppergrass grows as an annual on disturbed sites and dry open areas of Central Alberta. Its pinkish white flowers (2 to 3.5 mm long) bloom from **June through July,** appearing in racemes 5 to 15 cm long. It grows to a height of 60 cm and has numerous branches, lobed basal leaves and narrow, alternate stem leaves each with a few coarse serrations. The fruit appears as heart-shaped pods, 2 to 3 mm wide, each containing a single seed.

DID YOU KNOW...

The leaves of peppergrass can be used as a vegetable. They are a good source of potassium, phosphorus, calcium and Vitamins A, B and C. Seeds soaked in vinegar can be used as a seasoning for meat. A tea made from the plant was sometimes taken to treat kidney problems.

silverberry, wolf willow

Elaeagnus commutata

Bernh. ex Rydb.

WHERE, WHEN AND WHAT TO LOOK FOR

Silverberry, or wolf willow, grows as a shrub. It can be easily identified by its silver coloured leaves. It inhabits edges of aspen stands and overgrazed pastures. Its fragrant flowers are composed of 4 sepals, silver in colour on the outside and yellow on the inside. Petals are absent. Flowers appear in **May to June,** blooming inside leaf axils in clusters of 2 to 5. The purplish brown stem grows up to 4 m. Alternate leaves are 2 to 8 cm long and silver coloured on both sides. Silver berries, 1 cm in diameter, have tough skin and a mealy texture. Each berry has a single seed marked with 8 broad lines.

DID YOU KNOW ...

Native peoples ate silverberry only during food shortages, because the berries are edible, but tasteless. They cut the bark into strips to use as cord or rope, and they used the dried seeds as beads for necklaces and clothing decorations.

Canada buffalo-berry

Shepherdia canadensis (L.) Nutt.

male flowers

WHERE, WHEN AND WHAT TO LOOK FOR

Common in open woods and on riverbanks, Canada buffalo-berry can be found throughout Alberta. Male and female flowers appear on separate plants and bloom from **May through June.** Flowers have 4 brownish yellow sepals (2 mm across) and no petals. The shrub grows up to 3 m tall, with several stems arising from 1 rootstalk. Young shoots are scaly brown; older bark is greyish black. Oblong, opposite leaves, appear after the flowers, and they are 2.5 to 5 cm long, darkgreen on top and scaly brown underneath. The red berries, 4 to 6 mm in diameter, form in clusters around the stem.

DID YOU KNOW...

The common name, 'buffalo-berry,' was given by the Plains peoples. They believed that when the berries were ripe, the buffalo were fat enough to hunt. 'Soapberry' is another common name, because the juice of the berries contains saponin, a substance with a soapy flavour and texture. The fruit was added to buffalo meat for flavouring. It could also be whipped into a dessert Europeans called 'Indian Ice Cream.' Frost improves the flavour of the fruit.

pale coral-root
Corallorhiza trifida Châtelain

WHERE, WHEN AND WHAT TO LOOK FOR

Pale coral-root is a saprophytic herb favouring undisturbed, moist shaded areas in aspen and spruce forests. Pale, yellowish green flowers appear in **June** and can be recognized by their white 'lip,' which is often spotted with red or purple. The blooms (5 mm across) grow 3 to 12 per stalk. The greenish yellow stem grows up to 30 cm tall, has a coral-like, branched rhizome and no true roots. Leaves consist of 1 basal sheath and several yellowish green scales surrounding the stem. The fruit is a dry capsule containing many brown seeds.

DID YOU KNOW...

The genus name, *Corallorhiza*, refers to the coral-like rhizome of this plant. There are two other species of coral-root growing in Alberta (spotted coral-root, *C. maculata* Raf. and striped coral-root, *C. striata* Lindl.). These species are not as common as pale coral-root, have larger striped or spotted flowers and purplish or yellowish brown stems.

yellow lady's-slipper

Cypripedium calceolus L.

WHERE, WHEN AND WHAT TO LOOK FOR

Yellow lady's-slipper grows in moist areas along railway tracks, and on the edges of sloughs, peat bogs, moist woods and ditches. It is found at Wagner Natural Area and along the North Saskatchewan River valley. The pouch-like petal (2 to 4 cm long) is bright yellow with reddish purple dots. Sepals and remaining petals, greenish brown with purple stripes, are often twisted. Yellow lady's-slipper grows up to 40 cm tall, arising from a stout rhizome and coarse roots. Alternate leaves, 5 to 15 cm long, appear 3 or 4 per stem. The prominently-veined leaves are stalk-less, pleated and hairy. The fruit appears as a dry capsule with many small brown seeds.

SIMILAR SPECIES

Three other species of lady's-slipper are found in Alberta.

DID YOU KNOW...

This plant's genus name refers to the slipper of Aphrodite, Greek goddess of love. She was believed to have been born on the island of Cyprus; the name *Cypripedium*, means 'Cyprus foot.'

round-leaved orchid

Orchis rotundifolia

Banks ex Pursh

WHERE, WHEN AND WHAT TO LOOK FOR

In the Edmonton region, the round-leaved orchid can be found only in the Wagner Natural Area. It grows in mossy areas of moist spruce forests, a fragile habitat that does not recover readily from human disturbance. Its 2 to 8 pinkish white flowers have purple spots on their lips. A single basal leaf is about 3 to 7 cm in length. This little gem is often overlooked because of its size. The stem rarely exceeds 25 cm in height.

SIMILAR SPECIES

A related species, blunt-leaved orchid (*Habenaria obtusata* (Pursh) Richards.), can also found in the same habitat in the Wagner Natural Area. It has a single basal leaf and 6 to 15 green flowers.

DID YOU KNOW...

The habitat of orchids needs protection if wild orchids are to be preserved for future generations. Visitors to the Wagner Natural Area should stay on the hiking trails to reduce impact on the natural environment.

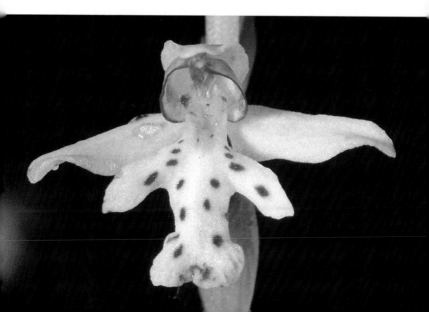

caragana, Siberian pea tree

Caragana arborescens Lam.

WHERE, WHEN AND WHAT TO LOOK FOR

Introduced from Siberia and Manchuria, the caragana, or Siberian pea tree, is now common throughout Alberta. Originally grown for hedges and windbreaks, it has established itself in the natural environment. Bright-yellow flowers (15 to 25 mm long) bloom in **late May,** emerging from scaly buds on slender flower stalks. The plant grows to a height of 4 m and has greenish brown bark. Alternate compound leaves with 4 to 6 pairs of oval, spine-tipped leaflets, appear in May. The fruit is a narrow pod, 4 to 5 cm long, that turns brown at maturity.

DID YOU KNOW...

In Siberia, farmers feed caragana seeds to their chickens. They also use the young pods as a vegetable.

peavine
Lathyrus ochroleucus Hook.

WHERE, WHEN AND WHAT TO LOOK FOR

Peavine inhabits aspen forests and margins of scrubland and it is found throughout our region. Clusters of 5 to 10 yellowish white flowers (each about 1.5 cm long) bloom from **June through July.** A climbing herb, peavine grows to a height of 1 m, grasping onto surrounding vegetation with modified leaf structures called tendrils. Alternate compound leaves have 3 to 5 pairs of oval leaflets, 2.5 to 5 cm long. The fruit appears as pods up to 4 cm long containing 4 to 6 seeds that are considered **poisonous** and should not be eaten.

SIMILAR SPECIES

A closely related species, wild peavine (*L. venosus* Muhl.), has purple flowers and 4 to 6 pairs of leaflets. It is found only in Central Alberta.

alfalfa

Medicago sativa L.

WHERE, WHEN AND WHAT TO LOOK FOR

Introduced from southern Europe as a forage crop, alfalfa is now widely distributed throughout Alberta. Dense clusters of 10 to 30 purple-to-blue (and sometimes whitish) flowers, 7 to 10 mm long, appear in **June.** The plant grows up to a height of 90 cm and has a deep taproot, allowing growth in drier areas. Compound leaves are alternate and have 3 minutely toothed leaflets, 1 to 3 cm long. The fruit is a hairy pod, 6 mm long, coiled 2 to 3 times, and containing 8 to 10 yellowish brown seeds.

DID YOU KNOW...

Alfalfa is used as a soil stabilizer to prevent erosion. Like most legumes, alfalfa has the ability to add nitrogen to the soil with the aid of certain bacteria. This process occurs in swollen parts of the roots called 'nodules.'

yellow sweet clover

white sweet clover
Melilotus alba Desr.

WHERE, WHEN AND WHAT TO LOOK FOR

White sweet clover was introduced to our region as a forage crop. Now common in Alberta, it inhabits roadside ditches and waste areas. White flowers (4 mm long) bloom from **June through August,** appearing in dense terminal spikes about 5 to 10 cm long. A biennial, the plant grows from a deep taproot to a height of 2.5 m. The fruit is a smooth pod 3 to 5 mm long containing 1 to 3 yellowish brown seeds.

SIMILAR SPECIES

A closely related species, yellow sweet clover (*M. officinalis* (L.) Lam.) has yellow flowers and a wrinkled pod.

DID YOU KNOW...

The young leaves and seeds of both species can be added to salads or cooked as a vegetable. When dried, the leaves have a vanilla-like flavour. Bees make excellent honey from sweet clover. This fragrant plant is often added to flower arrangements and satchets. Sweet clovers have been used in poultices and plasters to relieve rheumatism and other inflammations.

white sweet clover

79

golden bean

Thermopsis rhombifolia

(Nutt.) Richards.

WHERE, WHEN AND WHAT TO LOOK FOR

Golden bean, or buffalo-bean, a common plant of Central
Alberta, can be found in dry open areas. In the Edmonton area,
look for it in the Redwater sandhills. Golden yellow flowers (1 to
2 cm long) bloom from **May to early June,** appearing 10 to 20
per cluster. The plant grows up to 50 cm tall, often in large
patches. Alternate compound leaves have 3 oval leaflets, 2 to 4
cm long. The fruit is a brown, curved and twisted pod, 3 to 7 cm
long, covered in many grey hairs and containing 5 to 13 seeds.

DID YOU KNOW...

The flowering of the golden bean indicated to the Blood people
that the buffalo were fat enough to kill, hence its other common
name, 'buffalo-bean.' Some natives used a dye made from the
flowers of golden bean to colour skin bags and arrows. All parts
of this plant are **poisonous** and cause respiratory paralysis.

white clover

white clover, Dutch clover

Trifolium repens L.

WHERE, WHEN AND WHAT TO LOOK FOR

White, or Dutch, clover was introduced to our region from Europe in the early 1900s as a forage crop, but is now common in gardens, lawns, waste areas and roadsides. Its 15 to 20 whitish pink flowers (8 mm long) appear on short stalks in globe-shaped clusters that are from 1 to 2 cm in diameter. The compound leaves are composed of 3 leaflets, each about 2 cm in length. The plant's scientific name refers to its three leaves *(Trifolium)* and creeping nature *(repens)*. Fruit appears from June through August as pods 8 mm in length containing 2 to 5 seeds.

SIMILAR SPECIES

A closely related species, red clover (*T. pratense* L.) has pink flowers (12 to 20 mm long) that appear in larger clusters, 2 to 5 cm in diameter. Its leaves are somewhat hairy, and its pods are yellow to purple and 1-seeded.

DID YOU KNOW ...

Young white clover leaves contain large amounts of vitamins A, B, D, E, K, as well as some minerals. They make an tasty addition to soups, salads and cereals, but only in small quantities because they are difficult to digest. Dried flowers and seeds were used for breadmaking in times of famine.

red clover

wild vetch

Vicia americana Muhl.

WHERE, WHEN AND WHAT TO LOOK FOR

Wild vetch, a climbing herb growing up to 40 cm long, grasps onto surrounding vegetation with tendrils. It inhabits open grasslands and edges of aspen forests and can be seen throughout our region. Clusters of 3 to 9 purple-to-reddish purple flowers (each 1.5 to 2 cm long) bloom from **June through July.** Compound leaves are alternate with 8 to 14 oval leaflets, each 1.5 to 3.5 cm long and prominently veined. The pods, 2.5 to 3 cm long, contain 4 to 7 seeds.

SIMILAR SPECIES

A closely related species, vetch (*V. cracca* L.) is often found growing in the region. Its 1-sided flower clusters contain 15 to 40 bluish purple flowers.

DID YOU KNOW...

Seeds of this herb can be added to soups and salads. Dried seeds can be used as a replacement for caraway. Young stems can be baked or cooked as a potherb. Caution should be exercised when using this plant, because some sources indicate that the seeds may be **poisonous.**

habitat in September

tamarack, larch
Larix laricina (Du Roi) K. Koch

WHERE, WHEN AND WHAT TO LOOK FOR

Tamarack, or larch, is a deciduous conifer common in muskeg and swamp areas of Northern and Central Alberta. It grows up to 20 m tall and has pale-green, needle-like leaves (2 to 4 cm long) that appear in clusters of 10 to 20. The larches are unique among conifers in that their leaves turn brilliant yellow and shed in the fall. Cones are erect, 1 to 2.5 cm long and brown in colour, and they remain on branches until the following summer.

DID YOU KNOW…

The Cree boiled the inner bark and wood to make a poultice for healing frostbite and deep cuts. They chewed the resinous sap to relieve indigestion. They used the wood to make toboggans, and they used the rotten wood for tanning to give hides a yellow tint.

white spruce

Picea glauca (Moench) Voss.

WHERE, WHEN AND WHAT TO LOOK FOR

White spruce is common in Central and Northern Alberta. It grows up to 40 m tall in a variety of soils and habitats. Needle-shaped leaves appear 4-sided in cross-section and do not shed for several years. Drooping cones are 2.5 to 5 cm long and brown in colour. Cones have rigid seed scales. Seeds are dispersed in autumn, and the cones fall off during the winter.

SIMILAR SPECIES

A closely related species, black spruce (*P. mariana* (Mill.) BSP.), is the most common tree in muskegs and bogs. It grows up to 10 m tall. Most growth is in the top portion of the tree. Its cones are 2 to 3 cm long and stay attached to the tree for many years.

DID YOU KNOW ...

The Cree sewed birch baskets with small spruce roots. They made canoe paddles, fishnet floats and canoe ribs from the wood. Spruce sap can be used as chewing gum and was used as a sealant for birch bark canoes. The inner bark is said to reduce thirst, clean teeth and serve as an emergency food source. Needles and young twigs can be brewed into a tea.

jack pine

jack pine
Pinus banksiana Lamb.

WHERE, WHEN AND WHAT TO LOOK FOR

The jack pine is found on a variety of soil types, but grows best on well-drained, sandy soils. It grows to a height of 10 m. Needle-like leaves, 2 to 5 cm long, appear in groups of 2. Seed cones are 3 to 5 cm long and pointed toward the tip of the branch. They remain on the branches for several years. Bark is reddish brown and scaly.

SIMILAR SPECIES

A closely related species, lodgepole pine (*P. contorta* Loudon), grows to a height of 30 m, and has prickly seed cones that are at right angles to the branch. The lodgepole pine is the provincial tree of Alberta.

DID YOU KNOW...

Pine needles, young cones and inner bark are edible. The inner bark is rich in vitamin C and was eaten by European explorers to prevent scurvy. It was ground into flour or cut into strips and cooked like noodles. Young cones can serve as an emergency food source. A pleasant tea can be made from the needles.

lodgepole pine (mature cones)

saline shooting-star

Dodecatheon pulchellum

(Raf.) Merr.

WHERE, WHEN AND WHAT TO LOOK FOR

Shooting-star grows in wet areas, calcareous bogs and saline sloughs. It is common in Central Alberta. Flowers bloom in **late June,** appearing in numbers of 3 to 20 on flowering stems 5 to 50 cm tall. They are composed of 5 pink-to-purple petals curved backwards and 5 bright-yellow, fused stamens, giving the plant its striking colour contrast. Light-green, somewhat fleshy, basal leaves are spatulate and 4 to 17 cm long. The dry capsule splits into 5 sections, each containing many seeds 2 to 3 mm long.

SIMILAR SPECIES

A closely related species, mountain shooting-star, (*D. conjugens* Greene) is found in drier habitats at higher elevations.

DID YOU KNOW...

The genus name is Greek for 'twelve Gods,' the number of gods on Mount Olympus, who were said to revere this plant.

mealy primrose

Primula incana M.E. Jones

WHERE, WHEN AND WHAT TO LOOK FOR

Mealy primrose appears on the edges of sloughs, calcareous bogs and saline meadows. In the Edmonton area, it blooms in **late June.** Flowers (6 to 10 mm across) are pale lilac to pink with 5 petals so deeply notched that they look like 10. The stem reaches a height of 30 cm and is covered in a mealy white powder. Basal leaves, 2 to 6 cm long, are light green on top and powdery white underneath. The fruit is a capsule with many seeds, 0.5 to 0.7 mm in diameter.

sand heather

Hudsonia tomentosa Nutt.

WHERE, WHEN AND WHAT TO LOOK FOR

Sand heather, a shrub known in only 9 locations in Alberta, is found in sandhills near Redwater. Although limited to a few locations, it is common in those areas. Bright-yellow flowers (6 mm across) appear in **June** and are borne in loose terminal clusters. The 5 petals wither soon after flowering. A low-trailing shrub, 6 to 12 cm tall, it forms tufted bushes in sandy areas. Alternate leaves are 3 to 5 mm long, and they overlap each other like shingles. The leaves appear greyish green due to the presence of grey hairs.

saskatoon,
service-berry

Amelanchier alnifolia Nutt.

WHERE, WHEN AND WHAT TO LOOK FOR

Saskatoon grows at the edges of aspen forests and in dry open areas throughout Alberta. White flowers composed of 5 petals (9 to 20 mm long) appear from **May through June** and are borne in dense terminal clusters at the ends of the branches. The shrub grows to a height of 4.5 m, has rough, greyish brown bark, and alternate, oval-shaped leaves 1 to 5 cm in length. Dark-purple berries, up to 1 cm in diameter, appear in July.

DID YOU KNOW...

The nutritional value of the saskatoon has been known for centuries. Native peoples and European settlers used the plant as an important staple food. The Blackfoot mixed buffalo fat, blood and saskatoon berries and ate this as a favourite dessert. The berries were also a major ingredient in pemmican, and they were used to make a purple dye. The Blood people ground the roots to make a tobacco substitute. Nutritionists have determined that the fruit contains a high concentration of iron and copper.

round-leaved hawthorn

Crataegus rotundifolia Moench

WHERE, WHEN AND WHAT TO LOOK FOR

Round-leaved hawthorn grows on the south-facing slopes of the North Saskatchewan River valley and similar areas in our region. It inhabits the edges of aspen forests beside pincherry and chokecherry bushes. Clusters of 6 to 15 flowers (10 to 15 mm across) appear from **May through June.** The shrub grows up to 5 m tall, bearing stout thorns 2 to 7 cm long. Alternate leaves are also 2 to 7 cm long, round, with doubly serrated edges and shallow lobes. The red, berry-like fruit is 1 cm across and has several seeds and very little pulp.

DID YOU KNOW...

The fruit of hawthorn is high in sugar and low in fat and protein, and it **may be toxic** if consumed in large quantities. Native peoples ate boiled berries as a treatment for constipation, and they prepared a hawthorn tea as a stimulant. They made probes, awls and fish hooks from the sharp spines, and digging sticks and clubs from the hard wood.

woodland strawberry
Fragaria vesca L.

WHERE, WHEN AND WHAT TO LOOK FOR

Woodland strawberry can be found throughout our area. It grows up to 25 cm tall in moist, open woods and produces runners or stolons that form new plants. White flowers (approximately 2 cm across) appear from **early May through mid-September** and are composed of 5 petals with numerous yellow stamens at their centres. Basal compound leaves are composed of 3 leaflets.

SIMILAR SPECIES

A closely related species, wild strawberry (*F. virginiana* Duchesne) prefers open areas or forest edges. It also produces runners to form new plants. The terminal leaf-tooth of the woodland strawberry projects beyond the adjacent teeth, distinguishing it from the wild strawberry. Berries of both species are red, up to 1 cm across.

DID YOU KNOW…

Strawberries can be eaten fresh or cooked. A tea made from the fruit and leaves provides vitamin C and is said by some to be a tonic and stomach cleanser. A wash of berry juice added to water relieves reddened eyes and sunburns.

three-toothed cinquefoil

Potentilla tridentata Ait.

WHERE, WHEN AND WHAT TO LOOK FOR

The three-toothed cinquefoil grows in dry, sandy open areas in pine and spruce forests. It is found at the Redwater sandhills near Edmonton and in northeastern Alberta. Flowers (up to 2 cm across), consisting of 5 green sepals and 5 white petals, appear from **May through June.** Arising from a woody root-stalk, the plant can grow up to 30 cm in height, but it rarely exceeds 10 cm. Alternate, compound leaves (that appear basal) have 3 leaflets, each having 3 teeth. The species name tridentata means '3-toothed.'

There are 28 species of cinquefoil growing in Alberta, with 11 growing in the Edmonton and Central Alberta region. One species, shrubby cinquefoil, (*P. fruticosa* L.), is commonly grown as an ornamental shrub.

pincherry

Prunus pensylvanica L. f.

WHERE, WHEN AND WHAT TO LOOK FOR

Pincherry is a common shrub throughout Alberta. Although it prefers dry, sandy soils, it also grows on the edges of aspen forests. Clusters of 5 to 15 white flowers (each 12 to 18 mm across) appear in **May** at the same time as the leaves. Growing up to 8 m high, it sometimes appears as a small tree and can be identified by its smooth, purplish brown bark. Alternate leaves are 5 to 12 cm long with a red petiole and a margin of many fine teeth. Fruit appear on single stems in the form of small, bright-red cherries, 5 to 8 mm in diameter.

DID YOU KNOW...

The tart fruit of this shrub makes an excellent jelly. However, avoid the cherry pits, since they contain cyanic acid and are **potentially fatal** if eaten in large quantities. All parts of the pincherry, except the fruit, may contain hydrocyanic acid and may be **poisonous** if consumed. Native peoples used narrow strips of bark as rope.

chokecherry

Prunus virginiana L.

WHERE, WHEN AND WHAT TO LOOK FOR

Chokecherry, a common shrub on the edges of aspen forests and in dry open areas, grows throughout Alberta. Dense, cylindrical clusters of up to 35 white flowers (each 1 to 1.5 cm across) bloom from May through June. The shrub grows to a height of 5 m and has greyish brown bark. Alternate leaves are 2 to 8 cm long with finely serrated margins. Fruit appears as a small, purple-to-black cherry, 6 to 8 mm across.

DID YOU KNOW...

Although sour to the taste, chokecherries make delicious jams and jellies. The Blackfoot ground the entire fruit (pit included, although it is **somewhat toxic**) and formed dry cakes which they ate as trail food. They added ground berries to pemmican and fish. The Blood people boiled the fruit with blood as a treat. A strong, black tea made from the fruit was used as a treatment for coughs and colds. The Cree boiled twigs to make a tonic to relieve fever. All parts of the chokecherry, except the fruit, may contain hydrocyanic acid and may be **poisonous** if consumed.

prickly rose

Rosa acicularis Lindl.

WHERE, WHEN AND WHAT TO LOOK FOR

Prickly rose, the floral emblem of Alberta, is a prickly stemmed shrub that grows in woods and along roadsides and pastures. It is found throughout the province. Flowers (5 to 8 cm across) appear from **June through July.** They are deep pink to pale rose with numerous yellow stamens in their centres. Prickly rose grows to a height of 1.5 m. Alternate compound leaves have 3 to 7 oval, coarsely toothed leaflets. The red fruit (called a 'hip') is round to pear-shaped and contains several hairy seeds (achenes).

SIMILAR SPECIES

A closely related species, the Wood's rose (*R. woodsii* Lindl.), has a globe-shaped fruit and 5 to 9 leaflets. It has fewer thorns than prickly rose. The two species are known to hybridize.

DID YOU KNOW …

The rosehip has a high vitamin C content. Teas, jams and jellies can be made from the petals and hips of these plants. Some native peoples placed rose branches around the home of a deceased person to prevent the ghost from returning and haunting the home. Relatives of the deceased person also drank a tea made from the branches to protect themselves.

dwarf raspberry, arctic raspberry

Rubus arcticus L.

WHERE, WHEN AND WHAT TO LOOK FOR

Dwarf raspberry, or arctic raspberry, is a tiny plant that inhabits mossy lakeshores and wet, open areas in spruce forests. It is common in Central Alberta. Pink flowers (1 to 1.5 cm across) are composed of 5 petals and appear singly on each plant. The stem is usually less than 15 cm tall. The 2 to 4 compound alternate leaves have 3 leaflets, each 1 to 4 cm long. Fruit appears as a red berry similar to the raspberry.

DID YOU KNOW...

The dark-red berry is delicious and can be eaten fresh. The dried leaves make a pleasant tea.

red raspberry

Rubus idaeus L.

WHERE, WHEN AND WHAT TO LOOK FOR

Red raspberry is common throughout Alberta, growing in open aspen forests, burned-over areas, riverbanks and roadside ditches. White flowers (8 to 15 mm across) appear in terminal clusters in **early June.** A red berry, 1 cm across, ripens in July. The shrub grows to a height of 2 m with bristly, reddish brown stems, some of which last more than two years. Alternate compound leaves have 3 to 5 oval-shaped, crinkled leaflets, each 5 to 10 cm long.

DID YOU KNOW...

A tea made from the berries and leaves of this well-known plant is said by some to relieve morning sickness when taken during pregnancy. Warm tea taken during labour is said to have a relaxing effect. A poultice prepared from the leaves and fruit was used to soothe wounds, burns and insect bites. Raspberries are delicious eaten fresh; if picked in large quantities they can be made into jams and wine.

bishop's-cap

Mitella nuda L.

WHERE, WHEN AND WHAT TO LOOK FOR

Bishop's-cap grows in cool, moist spruce forests, often rooting in moss. It is common throughout the forested areas of Alberta. Greenish white, feather-like flowers (6 to 10 mm across) bloom in **June,** appearing on flowering stalks in groups of 3 to 10. The plant grows up to 20 cm , with long, creeping roots. Heart-shaped basal leaves, 2.5 cm across, have several stiff hairs on both the upper and lower surfaces. One small stem leaf is found below the lowest flower. The fruit contains small, black seeds, about 1 mm in diameter.

DID YOU KNOW...

Basal leaves are a common trait among members of the Saxifrage Family. The common name, 'bishop's-cap,' refers to the stiff, white hairs on the upper surface of the leaf. The Cree used the crushed leaves as a remedy for ear-aches.

leafy spurge, wolf's milk

Euphorbia esula L.

WHERE, WHEN AND WHAT TO LOOK FOR

Leafy spurge, or wolf's milk, is a deep-rooted perennial that grows in sandy roadside ditches and waste areas and on cultivated land. This weed is found throughout Alberta. Greenish yellow flowers appear in **late June.** Flower clusters have 4 crescent-shaped glands and are borne in 2 leaf-like bracts, 1 cm wide and 1.2 cm long. Male flowers have a single stamen; female flowers have a single pistil. Sepals and petals are absent. The greenish yellow plant grows up to 90 cm tall and has alternate leaves 2 to 7.5 cm long. The leaves below the flower often appear whorled. The fruit is a capsule 3 mm long which bursts open when ripe to release 3 seeds.

DID YOU KNOW...

Leafy spurge is a weed introduced from Europe and Asia. The milky juice of leafy spurge irritates sensitive skin and the digestive tract. This plant may be **toxic** and is not recommended for consumption. Legend says that the plant supplies the devil with milk.

round-leaved sundew

Drosera rotundifolia L.

leaf

WHERE, WHEN AND WHAT TO LOOK FOR

Easily overlooked because of its small size and inconspicuous flowers, with leaves the same colour as the moss in which it grows, the round-leaved sundew inhabits cold, black spruce bogs and can be found at Wagner Natural Area. The 3 to 10 inconspicuous, whitish pink flowers (4 mm across), appear in **July** on leafless flowering stalks. The plant grows up to 20 cm tall and has a basal rosette of 4 to 12 reddish green leaves. Leaves are 3 to 10 cm long and spoon-shaped. They are covered in sticky-tipped hairs to trap insects.

SIMILAR SPECIES

A closely related species, angle-leaved sundew (*D. anglica* Huds.) has longer, narrower leaves.

DID YOU KNOW…

The soil in which sundew grows is low in nitrogen and phosphorous. Its red, sticky-tipped leaf hairs attract and capture small insects that supply these nutrients. The hairs and leaf edges curl inward and surround the insect. After the plant has digested the insect, the leaf reopens and releases the skeleton. Sundews have been used in the treatment of whooping cough, bronchitis and asthma.

basal leaves

Western Canada violet

Viola canadensis L.

WHERE, WHEN AND WHAT TO LOOK FOR

The Western Canada violet grows in moist aspen woods and occasionally under spruce. Flowers (1 to 2.5 cm across) bloom from **June through August,** each appearing as 5 white petals with purplish veins and a yellow throat. The plant grows up to 60 cm tall, often forming large colonies from an underground root system. Alternate leaves are heart shaped, up to 10 cm across, and larger at the bottom of the stem than at the top. The fruit is a dry capsule 8 to 12 mm long with several short spines.

DID YOU KNOW...

This violet is prescribed by some herbalists for the relief of pain associated with cancer. Violet tea is a remedy for stomach and bowel complaints. The Blood people collected the flowers of a closely related species, the early blue violet (*V. adunca* J.E. Smith) to make a dye for colouring arrows.

balsam poplar

Populus balsamifera L.

male catkin

WHERE, WHEN AND WHAT TO LOOK FOR

Balsam poplar grows in moist areas in river valleys and forests. Male catkins are red; females are greyish white and borne on separate trees in **late April, before the leaves.** The alternate leaves are 8 to 15 cm long and have a shiny upper surface. The tree grows as high as 25 m with deeply furrowed bark. Sticky buds enclose the young leaves; they can be a nuisance in the spring, sticking to shoes, cars and pets. Small, green capsules containing small seeds and cottony hairs ripen in June.

DID YOU KNOW...

The primary method of reproduction in most poplar species is root suckering. The sap of all species of the Willow Family contains a chemical called 'salicin,' which is chemically related to aspirin. The Blackfoot made a tonic from the sap to reduce fever and headaches. They used an extract from the buds of balsam poplar to treat snow blindness, and to make perfume. They sometimes applied a poultice made from fresh leaves to sores.

leaf and bark

male catkin

trembling aspen, white poplar

Populus tremuloides Michx.

WHERE, WHEN AND WHAT TO LOOK FOR

Trembling aspen, or white poplar, is the most common tree in Alberta. Greyish white male catkins (2 to 4 cm long) and female catkins (4 to 10 cm long) are borne on separate trees in **late April, before the leaves.** Alternate, oval-shaped leaves are 4 to 7 cm long, with a dark green upper surface and a pale underside. The flattened petiole allows the leaf to move, even in the slightest of breezes—hence the name 'trembling' aspen. It grows up to 20 m tall with a trunk up to 60 cm in diameter. Bark is greenish white in younger trees, becoming furrowed with age. Fruit appears as small green capsules that split when mature. The seeds are covered in a cottony mass, prevalent in June and July.

DID YOU KNOW ...

The white powdery substance found on the tree trunks of trembling aspen can be used to stop cuts from bleeding. Fresh leaves can be crushed and applied directly to bee stings to reduce irritation. The dry, rotten wood of aspen was used to smoke whitefish and moose meat.

pink wintergreen

Pyrola asarifolia L.

WHERE, WHEN AND WHAT TO LOOK FOR

Pink wintergreen, common in aspen forests, is found throughout Alberta. Nodding pink flowers (1 to 2 cm across) appear 5 to 15 per stalk and can be easily recognized by their long, protruding styles. Flowering stalks often remain into the following summer. The plant grows up to 30 cm tall, often in small patches. Basal leaves are leathery (2 to 7 cm across), and they remain green and shiny throughout the winter. Fruit appears as a dry capsule which releases many seeds in late August.

DID YOU KNOW ...

Early botanists thought the leaves of pink wintergreen resembled those of wild ginger, hence the Latin name *asarifolia* meaning 'leaves that look like wild ginger.' Mashed leaves applied to an insect bite relieve pain and swelling. An infusion of the leaves was used by some to treat sore eyes.

Glossary

A C H E N E

   Dry, one-seeded fruit that does not open when ripe.

A N N U A L

   Plant whose life cycle is completed in one growing season.

A N T H E R

   The portion of the stamen that produces pollen.

A P E X

   Tip of a leaf or petal.

A X I L

   The angle formed between the leaf and the stem.

B A S A L

   At or towards the base of the structure

B I E N N I A L

   A plant that germinates one year, produces seeds the following year, then dies.

B R A C T

   Leaf-like structure found below a flower or flower cluster.

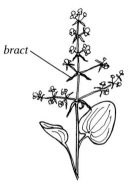

bract

C A L C A R E O U S

   Soils with a high calcium content.

C A L Y X

   Structure formed by the union of the sepals.

C A P S U L E

   A dry fruit that opens when mature.

C A T K I N

   Type of flowering stalk on which male or female flowers lack petals.

CLEFT
Deeply lobed.

COMPOUND LEAF
A leaf composed of two or more leaflets.

CONIFEROUS
Cone-bearing plants.

COROLLA
Structure formed by the union of the petals.

DECIDUOUS
Having leaves that fall in autumn.

DECOCTING
A process by which substances are extracted by boiling.

DISC FLORET
Small flowers, usually tube-shaped, in the Aster Family. *(see ray floret)*

DRUPELET
One part of an aggregate fruit, like those of raspberries.

EMERGENT
A plant whose stem rises out of the water.

FIBROUS
Thread-like roots of plants.

FRUIT
The part of the plant that contains seeds.

GENUS
(PL. GENERA)
A group of species having similar characteristics.

GLABROUS
Without hair.

GLAND
A structure that usually produces nectar or another sticky substance.

HERB
A plant having no woody stems.

INVOLUCRE
A bract or group of bracts below a flower cluster.

involucre

NODE
The point at which the leaf is attached to the stem.

NOXIOUS
A plant that may compete with agricultural crops.

NUTLET
A small nut.

OVARY
Part of the pistil containing the ovules.

OVATE
Egg-shaped and broader at the base, usually in reference to leaves.

OVULE
Undeveloped seeds, contained in the ovary.

PAPPUS
Hairs or bristles that are attached to the seed in the Aster Family.

PARASITE
A plant that obtains food and nutrients from another living plant.

PERENNIAL
A plant, or part of a plant, living more than two growing seasons.

PETAL
An interior, modified flower leaf, often brightly coloured.

PETIOLE
The stalk of a leaf.

PINNATE
Compound leaf with leaflets arranged on both side of the stalk.
(See illustration, page xiii.)

PISTIL
The female part of the flower, normally composed of the ovary, style and stigma.

POD
A dry fruit that releases its seeds when mature.

POLLEN
The male microspores of plants, usually resembling dust.

POULTICE
A moist mass of herbs applied to the body as external medicine.

PRICKLE
A spiny structure on the surface of a plant.

RACEME
    Flower cluster with flowers
    that bloom up from the
    bottom of the cluster.

RAY FLORET
    Strap-like, often marginal
    flower type in the Aster
    Family.

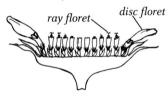

ray floret   *disc floret*

RHIZOME
    An elongated, under-
    ground stem.

ROSETTE
    A cluster of basal leaves.

SAMARA
    A dry fruit having wing-
    like structures.

SAPROPHYTE
    A plant that obtains food
    and nutrients from
    decaying material.

SEMI-AQUATIC
    A plant capable of living in
    water and on wet shore-
    lines.

SEPALS
    The outermost part of the
    flower; usually green and
    leaf-like.

SERRATED
    Leaf margin having jagged
    edges.

SHEATH
    The base of the leaf that
    surrounds the stem.

SHRUB
    Woody plant having many
    stems arising from the
    root.

SIMPLE LEAF
    A leaf with a single blade.

SPATHE
A large bract which enclosed a flower cluster.

SPATULATE
Spoon-shaped.

SPECIES
A group of similar plants capable of interbreeding to produce offspring like themselves.

SPORE
An asexual reproductive structure in ferns and fern allies.

SPUR
A slender projection from the corolla or calyx.

STALK
A stem; any supporting organ *(eg. petiole)*.

STAMEN
The male part of the flower, usually composed of an anther and a filament (stalk).

STAMINODE
A sterile stamen.

STERILE
A flower without functional reproductive structures.

STIGMA
The female receptive surface that pollen grains attach to.

STYLE
The elongated part of the pistil between the stigma and the ovary.

SUCKER
A plant that grows from the underground root of another plant.

TAPROOT
The main root, like those of carrots.

TENDRIL
A clasping or twining part of a leaf.

TERMINAL
The end of the stem or leaf.

THALLUS
Plants without differentiation between stems and leaves.

TREE

A woody plant having one
stem arising from the root.

TRUE FLOWER

Flower possessing stamens
and/or pistils.

UMBEL

Flower arrangement where
the flower stalks originate
from one point.

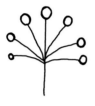

VASCULAR TISSUE

Specialized conductive
vessels in plants, used in
transportation of food and
water.

Bibliography

Alberta Agriculture. 1983. *Weeds of Alberta.* Alberta Agriculture and Alberta Environmental Centre, Edmonton, Alberta.

Angier, Bradford. 1978. *Field Guide to Medicinal Wild Plants.* Stackpole Books, Harrisburg, Pennsylvania.

Angier, Bradford. 1974. *Guide to the Edible Wild Plants.* Stackpole Books, Harrisburg, Pennsylvania.

Brown, Annora. 1970. *Old Man's Garden.* Gray's Publishing, British Columbia, Canada.

Burgess, Jean. 1980. *Walk on the Wild Side: An All Season Trail Guide to Elk Island National Park.* Friends of Elk Island Society, Fort Saskatchewan, Alberta.

Elliott, Douglas B. 1976. *Roots, An Underground Botany and Forager's Guide.* Chatam Press, Old Grenwich, Connecticut.

Fielder, Mildred. 1975. *Plant Medicine and Folklore.* Winchester Press, New York.

Forestry Branch. 1980. *Guide to Forest Understory Vegetation in Saskatchewan, Technical Bulletin No. 9.* Saskatchewan Tourism and Renewable Resources, Regina, Saskatchewan.

Gibbons, Euell. 1966. *Stalking the Healthful Herbs.* Alan C. Hood & Co. Inc., Pitney, Vermont.

Gleason, Henry A. 1963. *The New Britton and Brown Illustrated Flora of the Northeastern United States and Adjacent Canada.* Hafner Publishing Company, Inc., New York and London.

Jackson, Stephen, and Linda Prine. 1978. *Wild Plants of Central North America for Food and Medicine.* Peguis Publishers Ltd., Winnipeg, Manitoba.

Johnston, Alex. 1982. *Plants and the Blackfoot.* Natural History Occasional Paper No. 4, Alberta Culture, Edmonton, Alberta.

Kavasch, E. Barrie. 1981. *Guide to Northeastern Wild Edibles.* Hancock House Publishers Ltd., Vancouver, B.C.

Kindscher, Kelly. 1987. *Edible Wild Plants of the Prairie.* University of Kansas Press.

Langshaw, Rick. 1983. *Naturally: Medicinal Herbs & Edible Plants of the Canadian Rockies.* Summerthought Publications, Banff, Alberta.

Leighton, Anna L. 1985. *Wild Plant Use by the Woods Cree of East-central Saskatchewan.* National Museum of Man, Ottawa, Canada.

Looman, J., and K.F. Best. 1987. *Budd's Flora of the Canadian Prairie Provinces.* Agriculture Canada, Ottawa, Canada.

Michael, Pamela. 1986. *A Country Harvest.* Peerage Books, London, United Kingdom.

Moss, E.H. 1983. *Flora of Alberta.* Second Edition, rev. by J.G. Packer. University of Toronto Press, Toronto.

Porsild, A.E., and W.J. Cody. 1980. *Vascular Plants of Continental Northwest Territories, Canada.* National Museums of Canada, Ottawa, Canada.

Provincial Museum of Alberta. 1975. *Living with the Land.* Edmonton, Alberta.

Rogers, Dilwyn J. 1980. *Edible, Medicinal, Useful and Poisonous Wild Plants of the Great Northern Plains - South Dakota Region.* Buechel Memorial Lakota Museum, St. Francis, South Dakota.

Scoggan, H.J. 1978-79. *The Flora of Canada, vol. 1-4.* National Museums of Canada, Ottawa, Canada.

Stevens, E. John. 1973. *Discovering Wild Plant Names.* Shire Publications Ltd., Bucks, United Kingdom.

Sweet, Muriel. 1962. *Common Edible and Useful Plants.* Naturegraph Co., Hearldsburg, California.

Szczawinski, Adam F., and Nancy J. Turner. 1978. *Edible Garden Weeds.* National Museum of Canada, Ottawa, Canada.

Tanaka, Tyozaburo. 1976. *Tanaka's Cyclopedia of Edible Plants of the World.* Keigaka Publishing Company, Tokyo, Japan.

Tomikel, John. 1976. *Edible Wild Plants of Eastern United States and Canada.* Allecheny Press, California, Pennsylvania.

Turner, Nancy J., and Adam F. Szczawinski. 1978. *Wild Coffee and Tea Substitutes of Canada.* National Museum of Natural Sciences, Ottawa, Canada.

Turner, Nancy J., and Adam F. Szczawinski. 1979. *Edible Wild Fruits and Nuts of Canada.* National Museum of Man, Ottawa, Canada.

Vance, F.R., J.R. Jowsey and J.S. MacLean. 1977. *Wildflowers Across the Prairies.* Western Producer Prairie Books, Saskatoon.

Walker, Marilyn. 1984. *Harvesting the Northern Wild.* Outcrop Ltd., Yellowknife, Northwest Territories, Canada.

Index to Common and Scientific Names

About the Authors

France Royer

Richard Dickinson

*R*ichard Dickinson and France Royer have been working together since 1989. Richard graduated from the University of Alberta with a B.Sc. in Physical Geography, while France is a self-taught photographer. Together they operate a botanical and photographic service company.

Both authors live and work in Edmonton. When they are not working, Richard and France both enjoy traveling and exploring the diverse plant habitats of western Canada.

Richard and France also co-wrote the forthcoming book *Wildflowers of Calgary and Southern Alberta* and have further writing projects planned.

Wildflowers of Calgary and Southern Alberta

*T*his richly photo-illustrated companion to *Wildflowers of Edmonton and Central Alberta* covers the grasslands, foothills, coulees and wooded valleys from Red Deer to the Montana border, the eastern slopes of the Rockies to Saskatchewan.

Featuring more than 200 colour photographs, line illustrations, complete descriptions for over 100 plant species, identification keys and glossary, *Wildfowers of Calgary and Southern Alberta* is a handy field guide for beginner and intermediate naturalists.

Anyone who hikes, bikes, walks or travels through southern Alberta will enjoy this friendly, easy-to-use guidebook.

202 colour photos; $14.95; 0-88864-283-0
At booksellers everywhere, or call The University of Alberta Press at (403) 492-3662.